# Serving Those Who Served: Benefits for American Veterans and Their Families

Copyright Page

TITLE: Serving Those Who Served: Benefits for American Veterans and Their Families

1<sup>ST</sup> Edition

Copyright @ 2023



ISBN: 9798223907619

# Table of Contents

Serving Those Who Served: Benefits for American Veterans and Their Families

By Roberto Miguel Rodriguez

# Chapter 1: Introduction to Healthcare Benefits for American Veterans and Their Families

Overview of the Book

"Serving Those Who Served: A Comprehensive Guide to Healthcare Benefits for American Veterans and Their Families" is a must-have resource for veterans and their families seeking a comprehensive understanding of the healthcare benefits available to them. This book aims to empower veterans with the knowledge they need to navigate the often complex system and ensure they receive the care and support they deserve.

In this subchapter, we provide an overview of the entire book, giving readers a glimpse into the valuable information and resources that await them. We begin by outlining the importance of understanding the benefits available to American veterans, as well as the impact these benefits can have on their overall health and well-being.

The book is organized into several sections, each focusing on a specific aspect of healthcare benefits. We start by delving into the extensive range of benefits available to veterans, including medical, dental, mental health, and long-term care services. We provide a comprehensive breakdown of each benefit, explaining eligibility requirements, application processes, and how to maximize the benefits to meet individual needs.

Furthermore, we emphasize the importance of understanding the evolving nature of healthcare benefits for veterans. We highlight recent legislative changes, policy updates, and any new programs or initiatives that may affect veterans' eligibility or access to certain benefits. Our goal is to ensure that readers are up to date with the latest information, enabling them to make informed decisions about their healthcare options.

Additionally, we provide practical tips and advice on how to navigate the complex bureaucracy surrounding healthcare benefits. We offer step-by-step guidance on gathering the necessary documentation, completing forms accurately, and effectively communicating with relevant agencies and healthcare providers. We aim to simplify the process and alleviate any confusion or frustration veterans and their families may encounter.

Throughout the book, we include personal stories and testimonials from veterans who have successfully utilized various benefits. These anecdotes serve as inspiration and motivation, reminding readers that they are not alone in their journey and that there is hope for a brighter and healthier future.

In conclusion, "Serving Those Who Served: A Comprehensive Guide to Healthcare Benefits for American Veterans and Their Families" is a vital resource that equips veterans and their families with the knowledge and tools they need to access and optimize the healthcare benefits available to them. By empowering our readers, we hope to enhance their overall well-being and ensure they receive the care and support they deserve.

Understanding the Importance of Healthcare Benefits for Veterans and Their Families

Healthcare benefits are a crucial aspect of support for American veterans and their families. In this subchapter, we will explore the significance and impact of healthcare benefits, specifically tailored to meet the needs of veterans and their loved ones.

Healthcare benefits for American veterans encompass a wide range of services, including preventive care, medical treatment, mental health support, and rehabilitation. These benefits ensure that veterans receive the necessary medical attention they deserve, improving their overall well-being and quality of life.

One of the primary advantages of healthcare benefits is access to specialized care. Veterans often face unique health challenges due to their service, such as physical injuries, post-traumatic stress disorder (PTSD), and exposure to hazardous substances. Healthcare benefits provide them with access to healthcare professionals who understand these specific issues, offering specialized treatment and support.

Additionally, healthcare benefits extend to the families of veterans, recognizing the sacrifices they make alongside their loved ones. Dependents and survivors may be eligible for coverage under certain healthcare programs, ensuring that their medical needs are also met.

Furthermore, healthcare benefits play a vital role in early detection and prevention. Regular check-ups and screenings can help identify health issues early on, allowing for timely intervention and reducing the risk of complications. This proactive approach to healthcare is essential for veterans, as it enables them to maintain optimal health and prevent chronic conditions from worsening.

Mental health and counseling benefits are another crucial aspect of healthcare support for veterans and their families. The psychological toll of military service can be significant, leading to conditions such as PTSD, depression, and anxiety. Healthcare benefits provide access to counseling services, therapy, and support groups, helping veterans and their families cope with these invisible wounds.

In conclusion, healthcare benefits are of utmost importance for American veterans and their families. These benefits not only address the physical and mental health needs of veterans but also recognize and support the sacrifices made by their loved ones. By providing specialized care, early detection, and mental health support, healthcare benefits significantly enhance the well-being and overall quality of life for veterans and their families.

How to Use This Guide

Welcome to "Serving Those Who Served: A Comprehensive Guide to Healthcare Benefits for American Veterans and Their Families." This subchapter is designed to help you navigate through this book effectively so that you can make the most of the valuable information it contains. Whether you are a veteran or a family member seeking healthcare benefits or exploring other areas of support, we have compiled a comprehensive guide to assist you.

To begin, it is important to note that this guide is divided into various sections, each focusing on a specific aspect of benefits available to American veterans and their families. We have organized the content into the following niches, ensuring that you can easily find the information most relevant to your needs:

1. Healthcare Benefits for American Veterans: This section covers everything you need to know about healthcare services available to veterans, including medical treatment, access to VA hospitals and clinics, mental health support, and specialized care for service-related conditions.

2. Educational Benefits for American Veterans: Here, we outline the educational opportunities available to veterans, such as tuition assistance, vocational training, and scholarships, enabling you to make informed decisions regarding your educational pursuits.

3. Housing Benefits for American Veterans: If you are in search of information on housing assistance programs, home loans, or mortgage benefits, this section will guide you through the various options and eligibility requirements.

4. Employment and Career Benefits for American Veterans: Learn about the resources and programs available to help veterans transition into the civilian workforce, find employment opportunities, and develop a successful career.

5. Disability Compensation Benefits for American Veterans: In this section, we provide details on how to navigate the process of filing disability claims and accessing compensation for service-related disabilities.

6. Financial Assistance Benefits for American Veterans: Discover the financial aid programs and resources available to veterans and their families, including grants, loans, and other forms of financial assistance.

7. Mental Health and Counseling Benefits for American Veterans: Here, you will find information on the mental health services and counseling support available to veterans and their families, ensuring that you receive the care you deserve.

8. Burial and Memorial Benefits for American Veterans: This section covers the various burial and memorial benefits available to honor the service and sacrifice of veterans, including funeral arrangements, grave markers, and survivor benefits.

9. Home Loan and Mortgage Benefits for American Veterans: If you are considering purchasing or refinancing a home, this section provides comprehensive information on the VA home loan program and other mortgage benefits specifically designed for veterans.

10. Small Business and Entrepreneurship Benefits for American Veterans: For veterans interested in starting or expanding a small business, this section highlights the resources, loans, and mentorship opportunities available to support your entrepreneurial aspirations.

To make the most of this guide, we encourage you to explore the relevant sections that align with your specific needs and interests. Each chapter provides detailed information, eligibility requirements, and application processes, enabling you to take full advantage of the benefits available to you.

Remember, the purpose of this guide is to empower you and your family with the knowledge and resources necessary to access the support you deserve. We hope that this comprehensive guide will serve as a valuable tool and a roadmap to a brighter future for all American veterans and their families.

# Chapter 2: Healthcare Benefits for American Veterans

Eligibility Criteria for Healthcare Benefits

As veterans and their families, it is crucial to understand the eligibility criteria for healthcare benefits available to you. Access to quality healthcare is a fundamental right that every American veteran deserves. In this subchapter, we will discuss the eligibility requirements for healthcare benefits and how you can ensure you receive the care you need.

To be eligible for healthcare benefits, you must have served in the active military, naval, or air service and have been discharged under conditions other than dishonorable. This requirement ensures that those who have faithfully served our nation receive the necessary healthcare support. Additionally, certain National Guard and Reserve members may also be eligible if they were called to active duty by federal orders.

It is important to note that the eligibility criteria may vary depending on the specific healthcare program. The Department of Veterans Affairs (VA) offers various healthcare benefits, including VA health insurance, hospital care, and outpatient services. Each program has its own set of eligibility requirements, so it is essential to consult the VA's official website or contact your nearest VA facility for detailed information.

Furthermore, eligibility for healthcare benefits is not limited to veterans alone. Spouses, dependents, and survivors of deceased veterans may also be eligible for certain healthcare benefits. This includes access to VA health insurance, caregiver support, and mental health services. The VA recognizes the importance of supporting the families of veterans and strives to provide comprehensive care for all those who have served.

To ensure you receive the healthcare benefits you are entitled to, it is crucial to gather all necessary documentation. This may include your discharge or separation papers, known as DD-214, as well as any medical records related to your military service. These documents will help verify your eligibility and ensure a smooth application process.

In conclusion, understanding the eligibility criteria for healthcare benefits is essential for veterans and their families. By meeting the requirements and providing the necessary documentation, you can access the healthcare services you need and deserve. Remember to explore the various healthcare programs offered by the VA and consult their official resources to determine your eligibility for each specific benefit.

Enrollment Process and Access to VA Health Care

As veterans and their families, it is crucial to understand the enrollment process and access to VA health care. The Department of Veterans Affairs (VA) provides comprehensive healthcare benefits specifically designed for American veterans. This subchapter will guide you through the essential information you need to know about enrolling in VA health care and accessing the services you deserve.

The enrollment process with the VA is simple and straightforward. To be eligible for VA health care benefits, you must have served in the active military, naval, or air service and been discharged under any conditions other than dishonorable. Additionally, veterans with service-connected disabilities, former prisoners of war, and Purple Heart recipients automatically qualify for VA health care.

To enroll, you can apply online through the VA's Health Eligibility Center or visit your local VA medical center. The application will require personal information, military service details, and income information to determine your eligibility for specific benefits. If you need assistance with the application process, the VA offers a toll-free number to guide you through the enrollment process.

Once enrolled, you gain access to a wide range of healthcare services provided by the VA. These services include preventive care, primary care, specialty care, mental health care, and prescription medications. The VA also offers telehealth services, allowing you to receive healthcare remotely, which is especially beneficial for those living in rural areas or with limited mobility.

Moreover, the VA provides comprehensive healthcare benefits for veterans' families through programs such as CHAMPVA and the Civilian Health and Medical Program of the VA (CHAMPVA). These programs ensure that eligible dependents and survivors can also receive the necessary medical care.

It is important to note that while the VA strives to provide quality healthcare to all enrolled veterans, there may be limitations and waiting times for certain services. However, the VA continually works to improve access and reduce wait times to ensure veterans receive timely and efficient care.

In summary, enrolling in VA health care and accessing the services you deserve is a vital step for veterans and their families. By understanding the enrollment process and the comprehensive healthcare benefits available, you can ensure that you receive the care you need and deserve as a valued American veteran.

Primary Care Services for Veterans

One of the most significant healthcare benefits available to American veterans is primary care services. This chapter aims to provide veterans and their families with a comprehensive understanding of the primary care services they are entitled to and how to access them.

Primary care is the foundation of any healthcare system, and the Department of Veterans Affairs (VA) is committed to providing high-quality primary care services to veterans across the country. These services encompass a wide range of healthcare needs, including preventive care, chronic disease management, and acute illness or injury treatment.

Preventive care is a vital component of primary care services for veterans. Through regular check-ups and screenings, veterans can identify health issues early on and receive appropriate treatment. Preventive care services include vaccinations, cancer screenings, blood pressure monitoring, and cholesterol checks. By taking advantage of these services, veterans can maintain their overall health and well-being.

For veterans with chronic diseases, primary care services offer ongoing management and support. Conditions such as diabetes, hypertension, and cardiovascular diseases require close monitoring and specialized care. The VA provides veterans with access to healthcare providers who specialize in managing these conditions, ensuring that veterans receive the necessary treatment and support to live their lives to the fullest.

In addition to preventive care and chronic disease management, primary care services also address acute illnesses and injuries. Whether it's a common cold, a minor injury, or an urgent health concern, veterans can rely on primary care providers to deliver timely and appropriate care. By offering same-day appointments, the VA ensures that veterans receive prompt attention when they need it most.

To access primary care services, veterans must enroll in the VA healthcare system. This process is simple and can be completed online, by phone, or in person at a local VA facility. Once enrolled, veterans can make appointments with primary care providers at their nearest VA medical center or community-based outpatient clinic.

In conclusion, primary care services are a fundamental aspect of healthcare benefits for American veterans. By providing preventive care, chronic disease management, and acute illness or injury treatment, the VA aims to support veterans in achieving optimal health outcomes. Veterans and their families are encouraged to explore these services and take advantage of the comprehensive care available to them through the VA.

Specialized Care and Treatment Options for Veterans

In recognition of the immense sacrifices made by our brave veterans, the United States government has established a range of specialized care and treatment options to ensure their health and well-being. This chapter explores the various healthcare benefits available to veterans that cater to their specific needs, as well as other essential benefits that contribute to their overall quality of life.

Healthcare benefits for American veterans are comprehensive and cover a wide range of services. From preventive care to specialized treatments, veterans are entitled to receive medical assistance through the Department of Veterans Affairs (VA) healthcare system. This includes access to primary care physicians, specialists, mental health services, and rehabilitation programs. Additionally, the VA ensures that veterans have access to prescription medications, medical equipment, and prosthetics.

Educational benefits for American veterans are another significant avenue of support. The GI Bill provides veterans with the opportunity to pursue higher education or vocational training. Through programs such as the Post-9/11 GI Bill, veterans can receive financial assistance for tuition, books, and housing, empowering them to further their education and expand their career opportunities.

Housing benefits for American veterans are designed to provide stable and affordable housing options. The VA offers home loan programs that assist veterans in purchasing, building, or refinancing their homes. Furthermore, homeless or at-risk veterans can access support services, transitional housing, and rental assistance programs to help them regain stability and security.

Employment and career benefits for American veterans aim to facilitate their transition into civilian life. The VA offers vocational rehabilitation and employment services to veterans with service-connected disabilities, aiding them in finding suitable employment or starting their own businesses. Additionally, veterans receive priority consideration for federal job openings, recognizing their valuable skills and experience gained during their military service.

Disability compensation benefits for American veterans are crucial in ensuring that veterans receive financial assistance for disabilities resulting from their service. The VA provides compensation for disabilities incurred or aggravated during military service, as well as pensions for veterans with limited income and disabilities not related to their service.

Financial assistance benefits for American veterans extend beyond disability compensation. Veterans can access programs such as the Veterans Pension Program, which provides additional income support to low-income veterans and their families. Moreover, emergency financial assistance programs are available to veterans facing unexpected financial hardships.

Mental health and counseling benefits for American veterans are of utmost importance. The VA offers comprehensive mental health services, including counseling, therapy, and treatment for post-traumatic stress disorder (PTSD), depression, substance abuse, and other mental health conditions. Specialized programs are also available for veterans who have experienced military sexual trauma.

Burial and memorial benefits for American veterans honor their service even after their passing. The VA provides burial benefits, including a gravesite in a national cemetery, a headstone or marker, and perpetual care. Additionally, the VA offers memorial benefits such as memorial plot allowances and military funeral honors.

Home loan and mortgage benefits for American veterans are designed to facilitate homeownership. Veterans can take advantage of VA-backed home loans, which often provide more favorable terms and require no down payment. This benefit allows veterans and their families to achieve the dream of homeownership with greater ease.

Small business and entrepreneurship benefits for American veterans support veterans in starting and growing their own businesses. The VA offers resources, training programs, and access to capital for veterans interested in entrepreneurship. With these benefits, veterans can leverage their skills and experience to create successful ventures that contribute to the economy.

In conclusion, American veterans and their families are entitled to a wide range of benefits catering to their unique needs. From healthcare and education to housing and employment, these benefits aim to support veterans in every aspect of their lives. By taking advantage of these specialized care and treatment options, veterans can lead fulfilling and prosperous lives after their dedicated service to our country.

Prescription Medications and Pharmacy Services

In this subchapter, we will explore the various prescription medications and pharmacy services available to American veterans and their families. We understand the importance of accessible and affordable healthcare for our veterans, and this section aims to provide a comprehensive overview of the benefits and resources available to you.

As a veteran, you are eligible for a range of healthcare benefits, including prescription medications. The Department of Veterans Affairs (VA) operates a nationwide network of pharmacies, making it convenient for you to access the medications you need. Whether you require maintenance medications for chronic conditions or short-term treatments, the VA pharmacy services are designed to cater to your needs.

One of the key advantages of utilizing VA pharmacy services is the cost-saving benefits. The VA negotiates with pharmaceutical companies to secure discounted prices for medications, ensuring that you receive them at a fraction of the cost compared to other providers. Additionally, if you have a service-connected disability, you may be eligible for free prescription medications through the VA.

To access these pharmacy services, you can visit your local VA medical center or clinic. You can also request refills through the VA's online prescription refill system, saving you time and allowing for a more streamlined experience.

In addition to the VA pharmacy services, there are also community care options available. Through the VA's Community Care Network, you have the flexibility to receive your prescription medications from local pharmacies in your community. This program ensures that you have access to medications even if you live far away from a VA facility.

Furthermore, it is essential to be aware of the various resources and programs that can help you better understand and manage your medications. The VA offers medication counseling services to assist you in understanding the purpose, dosage, and potential side effects of your medications. Additionally, you can access educational materials and resources online or through your local VA facility to enhance your knowledge about your prescribed medications.

In conclusion, prescription medications and pharmacy services are an integral part of the healthcare benefits available to American veterans and their families. By utilizing the VA pharmacy services or community care options, you can access affordable and convenient medications. Don't forget to take advantage of the additional resources and programs offered by the VA to ensure that you have a comprehensive understanding of your medications.

Mental Health Support and Counseling Services for Veterans

Introduction:

Mental health is a crucial aspect of overall well-being, and veterans often face unique challenges that can impact their mental well-being. In recognition of this, the United States government provides comprehensive mental health support and counseling services for veterans and their families. This subchapter aims to provide an overview of the various mental health benefits available to veterans and how they can access these services.

Understanding the Importance of Mental Health:

The experiences of military service can often leave lasting emotional and psychological impacts on veterans. From combat-related trauma to the challenges of transitioning back to civilian life, veterans may face a range of mental health issues such as post-traumatic stress disorder (PTSD), depression, anxiety, and substance abuse. It is crucial for veterans and their families to recognize the importance of seeking help and utilizing the available mental health support and counseling services.

The Veterans Health Administration (VHA):

The VHA is the primary provider of mental health services for veterans and offers a wide range of programs and resources to address mental health concerns. These services include individual and group counseling, family therapy, medication management, and specialized treatments for PTSD and other mental health conditions. The VHA also operates Vet Centers throughout the country, which provide confidential counseling and support services specifically designed for combat veterans.

Accessing Mental Health Services:

To access mental health services, veterans can start by contacting their local VA Medical Center or Vet Center. These facilities will assess their needs and develop a personalized treatment plan. Veterans can also seek assistance through the Veterans Crisis Line, a 24/7 hotline that provides immediate support and connects veterans with local resources. Additionally, veterans may be eligible for mental health services through community-based organizations and nonprofit agencies that collaborate with the VA.

Support for Families:

Recognizing the importance of supporting the families of veterans, the VA offers counseling services for family members to address the challenges they may face. These services can help spouses, children, and other loved ones understand and cope with the mental health issues that veterans may experience.

Conclusion:

Mental health and counseling services play a vital role in the overall well-being of veterans and their families. By utilizing the resources and support available through the VHA, Vet Centers, and community organizations, veterans can access the care they need to address their mental health concerns. It is essential for veterans and their families to be aware of these benefits and to reach out for assistance when needed. By prioritizing mental health, veterans can enhance their overall quality of life and successfully navigate their post-service journey.

Rehabilitation and Long-term Care Services for Veterans

Chapter Overview:

In this subchapter, we will explore the range of rehabilitation and long-term care services available to veterans. We understand the unique needs and challenges faced by veterans and their families when it comes to healthcare, and this section aims to provide comprehensive information on the benefits and resources available to address those needs. Whether you require physical rehabilitation, mental health support, or assistance with long-term care, this chapter will guide you through the various programs designed to cater to veterans and their families.

# Section 1: Rehabilitation Services

Rehabilitation services are crucial for veterans recovering from injuries and illnesses acquired during their service. The Department of Veterans Affairs (VA) offers a range of programs, including physical therapy, occupational therapy, and speech therapy, to help veterans regain maximum functionality and independence. We will delve into the different types of rehabilitation services available, eligibility criteria, and how to access these services.

# Section 2: Long-term Care Services

As veterans age, they may require long-term care to ensure their well-being and quality of life. The VA provides a variety of long-term care options, such as nursing homes, assisted living facilities, and home-based care, to cater to the specific needs of veterans. We will discuss the different types of long-term care services, eligibility requirements, and how to navigate the application process successfully.

# Section 3: Caregiver Support Programs

Recognizing the critical role played by caregivers in the lives of veterans, this section will explore the caregiver support programs available through the VA. From respite care to training and education, these programs aim to support and empower caregivers in their role while ensuring veterans receive the care they need.

# Section 4: Specialized Rehabilitation for Mental Health

In addition to physical rehabilitation, veterans often require specialized support for mental health conditions such as post-traumatic stress disorder (PTSD) and traumatic brain injuries (TBI). We will discuss the various mental health rehabilitation programs offered by the VA, including counseling services, peer support, and residential treatment programs.

Conclusion:

Rehabilitation and long-term care services are an essential part of ensuring the well-being and quality of life for veterans and their families. This subchapter has provided an overview of the various programs and benefits available to address the unique healthcare needs of veterans. By understanding and accessing these resources, veterans and their families can receive the care and support they deserve.

Dental and Vision Care Benefits for Veterans

For veterans and their families, it is crucial to understand and take advantage of all the healthcare benefits available to them. Dental and vision care are often overlooked aspects of healthcare, but they play a significant role in maintaining overall well-being.

The Department of Veterans Affairs (VA) provides comprehensive dental care benefits to eligible veterans. These benefits include diagnostic, preventive, and restorative services such as cleanings, extractions, fillings, and dentures. Veterans can access these services through VA dental clinics or approved private dental providers. It is important to note that not all veterans are eligible for dental care benefits, and eligibility is determined based on factors such as service-connected dental conditions and disability ratings. However, all veterans enrolled in VA healthcare can receive one-time dental care if they have a service-connected dental condition or are scheduled for a VA-compensable service.

In addition to dental care, the VA also offers vision care benefits to eligible veterans. These benefits include routine eye exams, prescription eyeglasses, and medically necessary vision services. Like dental care benefits, eligibility for vision care benefits varies based on factors such as service-connected eye conditions and disability ratings.

It is essential for veterans and their families to stay informed about these benefits and understand how to access them. The VA provides resources and information on their website, including eligibility criteria, application processes, and frequently asked questions. Veterans can also reach out to their local VA healthcare facility or contact the VA directly for assistance.

Furthermore, veterans should be aware that there are additional resources available outside of the VA. Many nonprofit organizations and community clinics offer free or low-cost dental and vision care services specifically for veterans. These organizations often partner with local providers to ensure veterans receive the care they need.

Taking care of dental and vision health is crucial for overall well-being, and veterans and their families should not overlook these aspects of healthcare. By understanding their eligibility for dental and vision care benefits and accessing the resources available to them, veterans can maintain good oral and vision health, leading to a better quality of life.

In conclusion, dental and vision care benefits are vital components of healthcare for veterans. It is essential for veterans and their families to understand their eligibility for these benefits, access resources provided by the VA, and explore additional options available in their communities. By prioritizing dental and vision health, veterans can ensure they receive the care they deserve and maintain overall well-being.

# Chapter 3: Educational Benefits for American Veterans

GI Bill Overview and Eligibility

The GI Bill is a comprehensive program that offers a wide range of benefits to American veterans and their families. It was created to support the transition of veterans from military service to civilian life by providing educational, healthcare, housing, employment, and financial assistance benefits. This subchapter will provide an overview of the GI Bill and outline the eligibility criteria for each benefit category.

Educational Benefits: One of the most significant aspects of the GI Bill is the educational benefits it provides. Veterans and their families can receive financial support for college tuition, fees, books, and housing allowances. Eligibility for these benefits is generally determined by the length of service and the type of discharge received from the military.

Healthcare Benefits: The GI Bill also includes healthcare benefits for veterans and their families. These benefits cover a wide range of medical services, including preventive care, mental health counseling, substance abuse treatment, and hospitalization. Eligibility for healthcare benefits is typically based on the veteran's service-connected disabilities and income level.

Housing Benefits: Veterans and their families can also take advantage of housing benefits offered through the GI Bill. These benefits include home loans, mortgage assistance, and grants for home modifications to accommodate disabilities. Eligibility for housing benefits may vary depending on factors such as the veteran's length of service and the type of discharge received.

Employment and Career Benefits: The GI Bill provides numerous employment and career benefits to help veterans find meaningful employment and advance their careers. These benefits include job training, vocational rehabilitation, and assistance with job placement. Eligibility for employment and career benefits is often based on the veteran's service-connected disabilities and employment status.

Disability Compensation Benefits: Veterans who have suffered disabilities as a result of their military service may be eligible for disability compensation benefits. These benefits provide financial assistance to compensate for the impact of service-related disabilities on the veteran's quality of life and earning potential. Eligibility for disability compensation benefits is determined by the severity of the disability and its connection to military service.

Financial Assistance Benefits: The GI Bill also offers financial assistance benefits to veterans and their families. These benefits include grants, scholarships, and low-interest loans to support education, housing, and small business ventures. Eligibility for financial assistance benefits may vary depending on factors such as the veteran's length of service and income level.

Mental Health and Counseling Benefits: Veterans and their families can access mental health and counseling benefits through the GI Bill. These benefits provide support for mental health conditions, including post-traumatic stress disorder (PTSD), depression, and anxiety. Eligibility for mental health and counseling benefits is typically based on the veteran's service-connected disabilities and need for treatment.

Burial and Memorial Benefits: The GI Bill also offers burial and memorial benefits to honor the service and sacrifice of veterans. These benefits include burial in a national cemetery, a government headstone or marker, and a burial flag. Eligibility for burial and memorial benefits is generally determined by the veteran's military service and discharge status.

Home Loan and Mortgage Benefits: Veterans and their families can take advantage of home loan and mortgage benefits provided through the GI Bill. These benefits include low-interest loans, no down payment requirements, and mortgage assistance programs. Eligibility for home loan and mortgage benefits may vary depending on factors such as the veteran's length of service and income level.

Small Business and Entrepreneurship Benefits: The GI Bill offers support for veterans who are interested in starting or expanding their own businesses. These benefits include access to small business loans, training programs, and counseling services. Eligibility for small business and entrepreneurship benefits may vary depending on factors such as the veteran's length of service and business plan.

In conclusion, the GI Bill is a comprehensive program that provides a wide range of benefits to American veterans and their families. From educational and healthcare benefits to housing and employment assistance, this program is designed to support veterans in their transition to civilian life. Eligibility for each benefit category is determined by various factors, including the length of service, discharge status, and service-connected disabilities. By taking advantage of the opportunities offered through the GI Bill, veterans and their families can access the support they need to thrive in their post-military lives.

Types of Educational Assistance Programs for Veterans

As a veteran or a family member of a veteran, it is important to be aware of the various educational assistance programs available to you. These programs are designed to help veterans and their families pursue higher education and gain the necessary skills and knowledge for a successful career. In this subchapter, we will discuss some of the key types of educational assistance programs for veterans.

One of the most well-known educational assistance programs for veterans is the Post-9/11 GI Bill. This program provides financial support for veterans who have served after September 11, 2001, and covers the cost of tuition and fees, as well as a monthly housing allowance and a stipend for books and supplies. The Post-9/11 GI Bill also offers the option to transfer unused benefits to dependents, allowing family members to pursue their educational goals.

Another important program is the Montgomery GI Bill, which provides a monthly payment to veterans who have served at least two years on active duty. This program offers different tiers depending on the length of service, and veterans can use the funds to cover the cost of tuition, fees, and other educational expenses.

In addition to these federal programs, there are also state-specific educational assistance programs for veterans. Many states offer tuition waivers or reduced tuition rates for veterans who are residents of the state. These programs can significantly reduce the financial burden of pursuing higher education.

Furthermore, there are various vocational and technical training programs available for veterans who want to gain specific skills for a particular career. These programs often provide hands-on training and job placement assistance, helping veterans transition into civilian employment smoothly.

It is worth noting that educational assistance programs for veterans are not limited to traditional college or vocational training. There are also programs that support online education, distance learning, and apprenticeships, allowing veterans to pursue their educational goals in a flexible and convenient manner.

In conclusion, there are numerous educational assistance programs available to veterans and their families. Whether you are interested in pursuing a degree, learning a trade, or gaining specific skills, these programs can provide the necessary support and resources to help you achieve your educational and career goals. By taking advantage of these programs, veterans can enhance their employability, improve their earning potential, and successfully transition into civilian life.

Post-9/11 GI Bill and its Benefits

The Post-9/11 GI Bill is a comprehensive educational benefit program designed to support veterans and their families in pursuing higher education and career development opportunities. This subchapter aims to provide a detailed overview of the Post-9/11 GI Bill and its various benefits.

Under this bill, eligible veterans can receive financial assistance for tuition and fees, a monthly housing allowance, and a stipend for books and supplies. The amount of financial support provided depends on the length of military service and the type of educational program pursued. This benefit is not only available to veterans but can also be transferred to spouses or children, allowing them to access quality education.

One of the significant advantages of the Post-9/11 GI Bill is the provision of a Yellow Ribbon Program. This program allows veterans to attend private colleges and universities that may have higher tuition costs than the state-funded institutions covered by the bill. The Yellow Ribbon Program provides additional funding to bridge the gap between the tuition amount and the GI Bill benefit, enabling veterans to pursue education at their preferred institutions.

Moreover, the Post-9/11 GI Bill offers opportunities for vocational training, on-the-job training, and apprenticeships. These programs help veterans gain valuable skills and certifications in various fields, enhancing their employability and career prospects.

In addition to educational benefits, the Post-9/11 GI Bill provides housing benefits, including a monthly housing allowance. This allowance is based on the location of the educational institution and is intended to cover the cost of housing and utilities. This support ensures that veterans and their families can focus on their education without worrying about housing expenses.

To further assist veterans in their transition to civilian life, the bill also includes employment and career benefits. Veterans can receive career counseling, job placement assistance, and access to vocational rehabilitation services. These resources are tailored to help veterans identify suitable career paths and secure meaningful employment opportunities.

In conclusion, the Post-9/11 GI Bill is a vital program that offers a range of benefits to veterans and their families. Whether it is financial assistance for education, housing benefits, career development support, or access to vocational training, this bill is designed to ease the transition from military to civilian life. By utilizing the benefits provided under this bill, veterans can enhance their educational qualifications, improve their career prospects, and build a solid foundation for their future.

Vocational Rehabilitation and Employment Program

The Vocational Rehabilitation and Employment (VR&E) Program is a valuable resource available to American veterans and their families. Through this program, veterans who have service-connected disabilities or other barriers to employment can receive comprehensive support to enhance their employability and achieve meaningful careers.

The VR&E Program provides a wide range of services tailored to meet individual needs and goals. This includes vocational counseling, career assessment, and guidance to identify suitable employment opportunities. Veterans can also receive assistance in developing resumes, improving interview skills, and accessing job placement services.

One of the key components of the program is educational assistance. Veterans can receive funding for tuition, books, and supplies to pursue training or education programs that will lead to employment in a high-demand field. This support is especially beneficial for veterans looking to transition into civilian careers and acquire new skills.

In addition to educational benefits, the VR&E Program offers various resources to help veterans secure appropriate housing. This includes assistance with finding accessible housing options and support in obtaining home modifications to accommodate disabilities. The program also provides guidance on navigating the complex process of obtaining home loans and mortgages, helping veterans achieve their homeownership goals.

For veterans who wish to start their own small businesses or pursue entrepreneurship, the VR&E Program offers specialized support. Through business development assistance, veterans can receive guidance on developing business plans, accessing capital, and navigating the intricacies of starting and managing a successful enterprise.

Furthermore, the program recognizes the importance of mental health and counseling for veterans. It provides access to mental health services, including counseling and therapy, to address the unique challenges veterans may face. The VR&E Program also offers financial assistance benefits to help veterans overcome financial hardships and maintain stability during their vocational rehabilitation journey.

Lastly, the program ensures that veterans receive the recognition and support they deserve even after their passing. It offers burial and memorial benefits, including burial allowances, headstones, and markers, to honor their service and provide solace to their families.

The Vocational Rehabilitation and Employment Program plays a vital role in supporting American veterans and their families in various aspects of their lives. Whether it is healthcare, education, housing, employment, or financial assistance, this program is designed to empower veterans and help them lead fulfilling lives after their military service. By leveraging the resources and services available through the VR&E Program, veterans can take advantage of the opportunities and benefits they have rightfully earned.

Tuition Assistance Programs for Veterans

One of the most valuable benefits available to American veterans is the Tuition Assistance Program. This program provides financial support for veterans and their families to pursue higher education and skill development. Whether you are interested in obtaining a degree, attending a technical school, or acquiring new job-related certifications, this program can help you achieve your educational goals.

The Tuition Assistance Program offers a wide range of benefits, including funding for tuition, fees, and books. This means that you can pursue your education without having to worry about the financial burden of these expenses. Additionally, the program provides support for both full-time and part-time students, making it accessible to individuals with varying schedules and commitments.

For veterans who have already used their GI Bill benefits, the Tuition Assistance Program is an excellent resource to continue their education. It can be used in conjunction with other educational benefits to maximize your opportunities for success. This program is not limited to traditional college or university programs; it can also be utilized for vocational and technical training, as well as distance learning programs.

The application process for the Tuition Assistance Program is straightforward and user-friendly. You can apply online through the Department of Veterans Affairs (VA) website or seek assistance from a local VA office. The program is open to veterans who have served on active duty for at least 90 days after September 10, 2001, and have an honorable or general discharge. Dependents of veterans may also be eligible for these benefits.

Investing in your education can open doors to new career opportunities and increase your earning potential. The Tuition Assistance Program provides veterans and their families with the financial support they need to pursue their educational dreams. Whether you are interested in healthcare, business, or any other field, this program can help you achieve your goals.

In conclusion, the Tuition Assistance Program is a valuable resource for veterans and their families. It provides financial support for education and training, allowing individuals to pursue their educational goals without the burden of excessive expenses. Whether you are interested in obtaining a degree, attending a technical school, or acquiring new job-related certifications, this program can help you achieve success in your chosen field. Take advantage of this opportunity and invest in your future today.

Scholarships and Grants for Veterans

Education plays a crucial role in the lives of veterans as they transition back to civilian life. Thankfully, there are numerous scholarships and grants available exclusively for American veterans and their families to help them pursue higher education and achieve their academic goals. In this section, we will explore the various opportunities and resources available in the form of scholarships and grants for veterans.

The Department of Veterans Affairs (VA) offers several educational benefits, such as the Post-9/11 GI Bill and the Montgomery GI Bill, which provide financial assistance for tuition, fees, books, and housing allowance. However, there are additional scholarships and grants that veterans can apply for to supplement these benefits and further reduce the financial burden.

Many organizations and foundations across the country recognize the sacrifices made by veterans and offer scholarships specifically tailored to their needs. These scholarships can vary in terms of eligibility criteria, award amounts, and application requirements. Some scholarships are open to all veterans, while others may cater to specific branches of the military or service-related disabilities.

In addition to national scholarships, veterans should also explore opportunities at their chosen colleges and universities. Many institutions have their own scholarship programs exclusively for veterans, ensuring that they have access to the financial support they need to pursue their desired degrees.

To find scholarships and grants, veterans and their families can utilize online resources and databases that compile information on available opportunities. Websites such as Military.com, Fastweb, and Scholarships.com are excellent starting points for veterans seeking financial assistance for education.

It is important to note that the application process for scholarships and grants may require veterans to provide documentation of their military service, academic transcripts, letters of recommendation, and personal essays. Veterans should also be mindful of application deadlines and ensure they submit their materials in a timely manner.

By taking advantage of scholarships and grants, veterans and their families can alleviate the financial burden of higher education and focus on achieving their academic goals. These opportunities not only empower veterans but also acknowledge their service and sacrifice, ensuring they have access to the resources necessary for a successful transition into civilian life.

In the next chapter, we will explore housing benefits for American veterans, including assistance with home loans and mortgage programs designed specifically for those who have served. Stay tuned for valuable information on how to make homeownership more accessible for veterans and their families.

Education and Training Resources for Veterans

One of the most valuable benefits available to American veterans is the opportunity to pursue further education and training. Whether you're looking to enhance your current skills, switch career paths, or earn a degree, there are numerous resources available to help you achieve your goals. In this subchapter, we will explore the various education and training benefits that veterans and their families can utilize.

The Department of Veterans Affairs (VA) offers several programs to support veterans in their educational endeavors. The Post-9/11 GI Bill provides financial assistance for tuition, fees, and housing allowance for veterans pursuing higher education at colleges, universities, and technical schools. The Montgomery GI Bill is another option for veterans who served before September 11, 2001, and provides financial assistance for education and training programs.

In addition to these GI Bill programs, there are specialized educational benefits for veterans. The Vocational Rehabilitation and Employment

(VR&E) program assists veterans with service-connected disabilities in preparing for, finding, and maintaining employment. This program offers a range of services, including personalized counseling, training, and financial assistance to cover tuition, fees, and other necessary expenses.

For veterans interested in technical training or apprenticeships, the VA's On-the-Job Training program provides financial support to employers who hire veterans. This program allows veterans to earn a salary while receiving training in a specific trade or profession.

Furthermore, many colleges and universities have established programs and resources specifically for veterans. These include veteran resource centers, mentorship programs, and academic support services tailored to meet the unique needs of veterans transitioning to civilian life.

It is important for veterans and their families to be aware of the resources available to them when it comes to education and training. By taking advantage of these benefits, veterans can gain new skills, improve their career prospects, and ultimately enhance their quality of life.

In conclusion, education and training resources play a vital role in helping veterans successfully transition from military to civilian life. Whether it's pursuing a degree, vocational training, or on-the-job training, there are a variety of programs and benefits available to support veterans in their educational pursuits. By utilizing these resources, veterans can gain the skills and knowledge necessary for a successful career in the civilian workforce.

# Chapter 4: Housing Benefits for American Veterans

VA Home Loan Program Overview

The VA Home Loan Program is a valuable benefit available to American veterans and their families as part of the comprehensive range of benefits provided by the Department of Veterans Affairs (VA). This program aims to make homeownership more accessible and affordable for those who have served in the United States military.

The VA Home Loan Program offers several advantages over traditional home loans. One of the most significant benefits is the ability to purchase a home with no down payment, eliminating the need for a substantial upfront payment that can be a barrier for many individuals and families. Additionally, the program does not require private mortgage insurance (PMI), which can lead to substantial savings over the life of the loan.

Another key aspect of the VA Home Loan Program is its flexibility in terms of qualifying criteria. While traditional lenders may have strict credit and income requirements, the VA utilizes a more holistic approach to assess applicants' eligibility. This includes taking into account factors such as steady income, satisfactory credit history, and suitable debt-to-income ratios. These considerations make the program more accessible to veterans who may have faced financial challenges during or after their military service.

The VA Home Loan Program also offers assistance in refinancing existing mortgages. This can be particularly beneficial when interest rates are low, allowing veterans to potentially reduce their monthly payments or shorten the term of their loan.

It is important to note that the VA does not directly originate loans but instead guarantees a portion of the loan provided by approved lenders. This guarantee minimizes the risk to lenders, enabling them to offer more favorable terms and conditions to veterans.

To take advantage of the VA Home Loan Program, veterans and their families must meet certain requirements, including specific lengths of service and discharge conditions. The program is available for the purchase of primary residences, including single-family homes, condominiums, and manufactured homes.

In conclusion, the VA Home Loan Program is a valuable resource for American veterans and their families, providing them with an opportunity to achieve the dream of homeownership. The program's numerous benefits, such as no down payment and no PMI, make it an attractive option for those who have served in the military. By understanding the program's eligibility criteria and working with approved lenders, veterans can navigate the homebuying process with confidence and secure a stable and affordable home for themselves and their families.

Types of Home Loan Benefits for Veterans

One of the significant benefits available to American veterans and their families is the range of home loan benefits specifically designed to assist them in achieving their homeownership dreams. These benefits are aimed at making homeownership more accessible, affordable, and secure for those who have served their country. In this subchapter, we will explore the various types of home loan benefits available to veterans and their families.

1. VA Home Loans: The Department of Veterans Affairs (VA) offers VA home loans, which are backed by the federal government. These loans typically have lower interest rates, flexible repayment options,

and require little to no down payment. VA home loans are available for purchasing, refinancing, or building a home, making it easier for veterans to become homeowners.

2. Adapted Housing Grants: Veterans with service-connected disabilities can avail themselves of Adapted Housing Grants. These grants help modify an existing home or build a new home to accommodate the veteran's specific needs. This benefit ensures that disabled veterans can live independently and comfortably in their own homes.

3. Native American Direct Loan (NADL) Program: The NADL program provides home loans to eligible Native American veterans to purchase, build, or improve homes on federal trust lands. This program aims to improve access to safe and affordable housing for Native American veterans.

4. Interest Rate Reduction Refinance Loan (IRRRL): Also known as the VA Streamline Refinance loan, the IRRRL allows veterans to refinance their existing VA loan to take advantage of lower interest rates. This program helps veterans save money on their monthly mortgage payments, making homeownership more affordable in the long run.

5. Foreclosure Avoidance: The VA offers assistance to veterans who are facing foreclosure on their homes. They provide support, counseling, and options to help veterans avoid losing their homes and find alternative solutions to their financial difficulties.

These home loan benefits for veterans provide a pathway to homeownership and financial stability. Whether it's through lower interest rates, flexible repayment options, or assistance with modifications, these benefits are designed to make housing more accessible and affordable for those who have served their country.

In the next chapters, we will delve deeper into other crucial benefits for veterans and their families, including educational benefits, employment and career benefits, disability compensation benefits, financial assistance benefits, mental health and counseling benefits, burial and memorial benefits, small business and entrepreneurship benefits, and more. Through a comprehensive understanding of these benefits, veterans and their families can ensure they are utilizing the resources available to them and leading fulfilling lives after their service to the nation.

VA Home Loan Eligibility and Application Process

One of the most valuable benefits available to American veterans and their families is the VA home loan program. This program provides affordable mortgage options and a simplified application process, making homeownership more accessible for those who have served our country. In this subchapter, we will explore the eligibility requirements and step-by-step application process for VA home loans.

To be eligible for a VA home loan, veterans must meet certain criteria. First, they must have served a minimum of 90 consecutive days on active duty during wartime or 181 days during peacetime. National Guard and Reserve members may also be eligible if they have completed at least six years of service. Spouses of veterans who died in the line of duty or as a result of a service-connected disability may also be eligible.

Once eligibility is established, veterans can begin the application process for a VA home loan. The first step is to obtain a Certificate of Eligibility (COE) from the Department of Veterans Affairs. This document verifies the veteran's eligibility for the loan program. It can be obtained online through the eBenefits portal or by submitting a paper application.

After obtaining the COE, veterans can start searching for a home and find a lender who participates in the VA home loan program. It is important to choose a lender who is knowledgeable about VA loans and can guide the veteran through the process. The lender will review the veteran's financial information and determine the loan amount they qualify for.

Once a home is selected and the purchase contract is signed, the lender will order a VA appraisal to ensure the property meets the VA's minimum property requirements. If the appraisal is satisfactory, the lender will proceed with underwriting and finalizing the loan.

The VA home loan program offers numerous benefits, including no down payment requirement, competitive interest rates, and no private mortgage insurance. It is designed to make homeownership more affordable and accessible for veterans and their families.

In conclusion, the VA home loan program provides a unique opportunity for veterans and their families to achieve the dream of homeownership. By understanding the eligibility requirements and following the application process, veterans can take advantage of this valuable benefit. Whether it's purchasing a new home or refinancing an existing mortgage, the VA home loan program offers a range of options to suit the needs of American veterans and their families.

Homeless Veterans Assistance Programs

In the United States, it is a sad reality that many veterans find themselves without a place to call home. The transition from military service to civilian life can be challenging, and some veterans face additional obstacles that lead to homelessness. However, there are numerous assistance programs available to support homeless veterans and help them regain stability in their lives.

One vital program is the Homeless Veterans Assistance Program (HVAP), which is part of the U.S. Department of Veterans Affairs (VA). HVAP provides a range of services to homeless veterans, including outreach, healthcare, case management, and housing assistance. The program aims to connect veterans with the resources they need to overcome homelessness and reintegrate into society.

Homeless veterans can access comprehensive healthcare benefits through the VA. These benefits include medical, dental, and mental health services, ensuring that veterans receive the care they require to address any physical or mental health issues that may have contributed to their homelessness. The VA also offers specialized programs for veterans struggling with substance abuse or post-traumatic stress disorder (PTSD).

To address the immediate housing needs of homeless veterans, the VA operates several programs. The Grant and Per Diem (GPD) program provides funding to community organizations that offer transitional housing and supportive services to homeless veterans. Additionally, the VA's Supportive Services for Veteran Families (SSVF) program provides temporary financial assistance to veterans and their families to secure stable housing.

Employment and career benefits are crucial to helping homeless veterans regain independence. The VA offers job placement services, vocational rehabilitation, and education and training opportunities. By acquiring new skills, homeless veterans can improve their employability and secure sustainable employment.

Homeless veterans may also be eligible for disability compensation benefits. The VA provides compensation for service-connected disabilities that impede their ability to work or perform daily activities. These benefits can provide financial stability and support veterans in their journey toward self-sufficiency.

Mental health and counseling benefits are essential for homeless veterans who may be dealing with trauma, depression, or other mental health issues. The VA offers a wide range of mental health services, including individual and group therapy, substance abuse treatment, and support for families and caregivers.

When a homeless veteran passes away, the VA ensures they receive proper burial and memorial benefits. These benefits may include a gravesite, a headstone or marker, a Presidential Memorial Certificate, and burial allowances.

The VA also offers home loan and mortgage benefits to help homeless veterans achieve homeownership. Veterans can take advantage of low-interest loans, refinancing options, and mortgage assistance programs, enabling them to secure stable housing and build a foundation for their future.

For homeless veterans interested in starting their own businesses, the VA provides small business and entrepreneurship benefits. These benefits include access to loans, mentorship programs, and resources to help veterans succeed in the competitive business world.

In conclusion, homeless veterans assistance programs aim to provide comprehensive support to veterans experiencing homelessness. From healthcare and housing assistance to employment and financial benefits, these programs ensure that our nation's heroes receive the assistance they need to regain stability and lead fulfilling lives. If you or someone you know is a homeless veteran, reach out to the VA to explore the available resources and take the first step toward a brighter future.

Adapted Housing Grants for Veterans with Disabilities

One of the essential benefits available to American veterans with disabilities is the Adapted Housing Grant. This grant program provides financial assistance to veterans with service-connected disabilities, enabling them to modify or adapt their homes to meet their specific needs.

The primary aim of the Adapted Housing Grant is to enhance the quality of life for veterans by removing barriers and creating a safe and accessible living environment. Whether it is installing wheelchair ramps, widening doorways, or adding handrails, these modifications can significantly improve a veteran's ability to navigate their home independently and comfortably.

There are three types of Adapted Housing Grants available: the Specially Adapted Housing (SAH) Grant, the Special Housing Adaptation (SHA) Grant, and the Temporary Residence Adaptation (TRA) Grant.

The SAH Grant is designed for veterans with severe service-connected disabilities, such as the loss of multiple limbs or blindness. This grant provides funding to construct a new home or adapt an existing property to meet the veteran's specific needs. The maximum amount awarded under the SAH Grant is adjusted annually and can be used towards the cost of land, construction, or the payoff of an existing mortgage.

The SHA Grant is available to veterans with service-connected disabilities that are less severe but still impact their daily lives. This grant provides funding for modifications such as the installation of wheelchair-accessible bathrooms, handrails, or the expansion of living spaces. Like the SAH Grant, the maximum amount awarded under the SHA Grant is adjusted annually.

The TRA Grant is designed to help veterans adapt the residence of a family member temporarily. This grant is available to veterans who are temporarily residing in a family member's home and require modifications to improve accessibility.

To apply for an Adapted Housing Grant, veterans must complete the appropriate application form, which can be obtained from the Department of Veterans Affairs (VA). The VA also requires supporting documentation, such as medical records and evidence of the disability's service connection.

In conclusion, the Adapted Housing Grant program provides essential financial assistance to American veterans with disabilities, allowing them to modify their homes to meet their specific needs. Whether it is constructing a new home or adapting an existing property, these grants play a pivotal role in improving the quality of life for veterans and their families. If you or a loved one is a veteran with a service-connected disability, exploring the Adapted Housing Grant program is a crucial step towards creating a safe and accessible living environment.

Rental and Housing Assistance Programs for Veterans

One of the most critical aspects of a veteran's life is finding stable housing. Recognizing this, the government has implemented various rental and housing assistance programs specifically geared towards veterans and their families. These programs aim to ensure that veterans have access to safe and affordable housing options.

One such program is the Veterans Affairs Supportive Housing (VASH) program. This initiative provides rental assistance vouchers to veterans who are experiencing homelessness or are at risk of becoming homeless. Through partnerships between the Department of Veterans Affairs (VA) and local public housing agencies, eligible veterans receive rental subsidies, case management, and access to supportive services to help them maintain stable housing.

Additionally, the HUD-VASH program combines rental assistance from the Department of Housing and Urban Development (HUD) with VA supportive services. This collaboration helps veterans with mental health issues, substance abuse disorders, or other disabilities to secure affordable housing while receiving the necessary support to address their needs.

Another valuable resource for veterans is the Section 8 Housing Choice Voucher Program. Administered by HUD, this program provides rental assistance to low-income individuals and families, including veterans. Veterans can apply for these vouchers, which allow them to choose their housing while receiving financial support to cover a portion of their rent.

Furthermore, the VA provides grants to eligible veterans with service-connected disabilities to adapt their homes through the Specially Adapted Housing (SAH) program. This program assists veterans with severe disabilities by providing funds to modify their homes, making them accessible and accommodating to their unique needs.

In addition to these federal programs, various nonprofit organizations and charities offer rental and housing assistance to veterans. These organizations work tirelessly to ensure that veterans have access to safe and stable housing options by offering rental subsidies, transitional housing, and emergency shelter services.

For veterans and their families, it is essential to explore all available options for rental and housing assistance. By understanding the various programs and resources available, veterans can find the support they need to secure affordable and suitable housing. Whether through government programs or nonprofit organizations, veterans can find the assistance necessary to improve their housing situations and build a stable future for themselves and their loved ones.

Home Modification and Accessibility Benefits for Veterans

As veterans and their families, it is essential to be aware of the various healthcare benefits available to you. One crucial aspect of these benefits is home modification and accessibility, which aims to improve the living conditions of veterans with disabilities or mobility issues. By understanding and utilizing these benefits, veterans can enhance their quality of life and maintain their independence within the comfort of their own homes.

Home modification benefits for American veterans are designed to make necessary changes to accommodate disabilities or physical limitations. These modifications can include ramp installations, widening doorways, installing grab bars, and making bathroom and kitchen renovations. By ensuring that your living environment is adapted to your specific needs, you can navigate your home safely and comfortably.

Accessibility benefits go hand in hand with home modifications, as they focus on providing aids and equipment that promote independence and mobility. Veterans may be eligible for assistive devices such as wheelchairs, stair lifts, and specialized beds. Additionally, accessibility benefits may cover the cost of vehicle modifications, making transportation more accessible for veterans with disabilities.

These benefits are not limited to physical modifications alone; they also extend to adaptive technology. Veterans can receive assistive devices like voice-activated smart home systems, which allow them to control various aspects of their homes, such as lighting, temperature, and security, using voice commands. These technologies not only enhance convenience but also offer a sense of empowerment and autonomy.

To access these benefits, veterans and their families can consult the Department of Veterans Affairs (VA) or reach out to veteran service organizations for guidance. It is crucial to understand the eligibility criteria and documentation requirements to ensure a smooth application process.

By availing themselves of home modification and accessibility benefits, veterans can create a safe and comfortable living environment that caters to their unique needs. These modifications and aids not only enhance their daily lives but also foster a greater sense of independence and self-sufficiency.

In conclusion, home modification and accessibility benefits for American veterans are a crucial aspect of healthcare benefits. By understanding and utilizing these benefits, veterans and their families can improve their living conditions, maintain their independence, and enhance their overall quality of life. By taking advantage of these resources, veterans can ensure that their homes are adapted to their specific needs, allowing them to live comfortably and safely.

# Chapter 5: Employment and Career Benefits for American Veterans

Transition Assistance Programs for Veterans

Transitioning from military service to civilian life can be a challenging and overwhelming process for veterans and their families. However, there are numerous transition assistance programs available to help ease this transition and provide support in various aspects of life. This subchapter will delve into the different programs that are designed to assist veterans in areas such as healthcare, education, housing, employment, disability compensation, financial assistance, mental health and counseling, burial and memorial benefits, home loans and mortgages, as well as small business and entrepreneurship.

Healthcare benefits for American veterans are an essential aspect of transitioning to civilian life. The Department of Veterans Affairs (VA) offers comprehensive healthcare services to eligible veterans, including primary care, mental health care, specialized care for women veterans, and access to a network of VA medical facilities across the country. These programs ensure that veterans and their families have access to the healthcare they need to maintain their well-being.

Educational benefits for American veterans are also crucial in helping them pursue their educational goals. The GI Bill provides financial assistance for veterans to pursue higher education, vocational training, and apprenticeships. This program not only covers tuition fees but also offers a monthly housing allowance and a stipend for books and supplies, making education more affordable for veterans.

Housing benefits for American veterans provide assistance in finding suitable housing options. The VA offers home loans and mortgage benefits that include low-interest rates and no down payment requirements, making homeownership more accessible. Additionally, the VA also provides grants for disabled veterans to modify their homes to accommodate their specific needs.

Employment and career benefits for American veterans aim to help veterans find meaningful employment after their military service. The VA offers various programs such as the Veterans Employment Center, which connects veterans with job opportunities, career counseling, and resume-building services. Additionally, the VA's Vocational Rehabilitation and Employment program provides job training and support for veterans with service-connected disabilities.

Disability compensation benefits for American veterans ensure that veterans who have sustained service-related disabilities are adequately compensated. The VA provides disability compensation, which is a tax-free monetary benefit, to veterans who have disabilities resulting from their military service. This program helps veterans receive the financial support they need to cope with their disabilities and improve their quality of life.

Financial assistance benefits for American veterans encompass programs that provide financial support to veterans who may be facing financial hardships. The VA offers programs such as the Veterans Pension and the Aid and Attendance Benefit, which provide additional financial assistance to eligible veterans and their surviving spouses who need help with daily activities or require nursing home care.

Mental health and counseling benefits for American veterans address the unique mental health challenges veterans may face. The VA offers a range of mental health services, including counseling, therapy, and treatment for conditions such as post-traumatic stress disorder (PTSD), depression, and substance abuse. These programs aim to provide veterans with the necessary support and resources to maintain good mental health and overall well-being.

Burial and memorial benefits for American veterans honor the service and sacrifice of veterans who have passed away. The VA provides burial benefits, including a gravesite in a national cemetery, a headstone or marker, and a burial flag. Additionally, the VA offers memorial benefits such as Presidential Memorial Certificates and Military Funeral Honors to commemorate the veteran's service.

Home loan and mortgage benefits for American veterans assist veterans in achieving homeownership. The VA offers home loans with favorable terms, including low-interest rates, no down payment requirements, and no mortgage insurance premiums. These benefits make it easier for veterans to secure affordable housing and achieve the dream of homeownership.

Small business and entrepreneurship benefits for American veterans support veterans who wish to start their own businesses. The Small Business Administration (SBA) offers various programs and resources specifically tailored to veterans, including business loans, training programs, mentorship opportunities, and procurement assistance. These programs help veterans leverage their unique skills and experiences to succeed in the business world.

In conclusion, transition assistance programs for veterans play a vital role in supporting veterans and their families as they navigate the complexities of transitioning to civilian life. From healthcare and education to housing, employment, disability compensation, financial assistance, mental health, burial and memorial benefits, home loans, and small business support, these programs ensure that veterans receive the support they need to thrive in their post-military lives.

Job Placement and Training Services for Veterans

One crucial aspect of ensuring the successful transition of American veterans into civilian life is providing them with job placement and training services. Veterans possess a unique set of skills and experiences that can greatly benefit the workforce, but they often face challenges in translating their military experience into the civilian job market. This subchapter aims to provide veterans and their families with a comprehensive understanding of the job placement and training services available to them.

Job placement services for veterans are designed to assist in finding suitable employment opportunities that align with their skills, interests, and experience. These services typically include job fairs, resume writing workshops, interview preparation, and networking events. By connecting veterans with potential employers and equipping them with the necessary tools to market themselves effectively, these services increase the likelihood of successful job placements.

Training services for veterans focus on enhancing their existing skills or providing them with new skills and certifications required by various industries. Many organizations offer vocational training programs, apprenticeships, and on-the-job training opportunities specifically tailored to veterans. These programs help veterans acquire the qualifications necessary to enter high-demand fields such as healthcare, technology, and skilled trades. Additionally, educational benefits for veterans, such as the GI Bill, can be utilized to pursue higher education and obtain degrees that further enhance their career prospects.

It is important for veterans and their families to be aware of the various job placement and training services available to them. The Department of Veterans Affairs (VA) provides resources through its Vocational Rehabilitation and Employment (VR&E) program, which offers career counseling, job placement assistance, and educational support. Additionally, nonprofit organizations like Hire Heroes USA and the Wounded Warrior Project offer comprehensive job placement and training services exclusively for veterans.

By utilizing these services, veterans can overcome the challenges they may face during the transition from military to civilian life. Veterans and their families should take advantage of the available resources to ensure a smooth and successful transition into the workforce. Whether it is finding a job that aligns with their skills and interests or obtaining the necessary training to pursue a new career path, these services are integral in supporting veterans as they embark on the next chapter of their lives.

In conclusion, job placement and training services are vital components of the comprehensive support system for American veterans and their families. With the right resources and assistance, veterans can overcome barriers and achieve meaningful employment opportunities. By recognizing the unique skills and experiences veterans bring to the table, employers can benefit from a diverse and talented workforce. It is essential for veterans and their families to explore the job placement and training services available to them, ensuring a successful transition and fulfilling career after their service.

Federal Hiring Preferences for Veterans

One of the many benefits that veterans and their families can access is the federal hiring preference for veterans. This preference ensures that those who have served in the military are given priority consideration for employment opportunities within the federal government. This subchapter will explore the details of this preference and how it can benefit veterans in their search for meaningful employment.

The federal government recognizes the valuable skills and experiences that veterans bring to the workforce. As a result, it has implemented hiring preferences to give them an advantage in the competitive job market. Veterans who have been honorably discharged and meet certain criteria are eligible for these preferences.

Under the preference system, veterans are given priority over non-veterans when applying for federal job openings. This means that if a veteran and a non-veteran have the same qualifications for a position, the veteran will be given preference and have a higher chance of being selected for the job. This preferential treatment extends to all levels of the federal government, from entry-level positions to high-level executive roles.

To take advantage of this preference, veterans must provide proof of their military service, such as a DD-214 form, when applying for federal jobs. It is important for veterans to highlight their military experience and transferable skills on their resumes and during interviews. This will help federal hiring managers recognize the value that veterans can bring to their organizations.

The federal government also offers additional support to veterans seeking federal employment. This includes resources such as job search assistance, resume writing workshops, and interview preparation. These services are designed to help veterans navigate the federal hiring process and increase their chances of securing a federal job.

By taking advantage of the federal hiring preference for veterans, veterans and their families can open doors to a wide range of employment opportunities within the federal government. Whether it is in healthcare, education, housing, or entrepreneurship, veterans can find meaningful careers that utilize their unique skills and experiences. This preference is a way for the government to honor the sacrifice and dedication of those who have served our country, providing them with a pathway to successful civilian careers.

Vocational Rehabilitation and Employment Services

One of the most valuable benefits available to American veterans and their families is the Vocational Rehabilitation and Employment

(VR&E) program. This program, provided by the Department of Veterans Affairs (VA), aims to assist veterans with service-connected disabilities in finding meaningful employment and achieving their career goals.

The VR&E program offers a wide range of services and resources designed to enhance veterans' employability. These services include career counseling, vocational training, job placement assistance, and assistance with resume writing and interview skills. Through personalized assistance, veterans can identify their skills and interests, explore career options, and develop a plan to achieve their employment goals.

For veterans who require additional education or training to enter or re-enter the workforce, the VR&E program may provide financial support for tuition, books, and supplies. This can be particularly beneficial for those who wish to pursue a new career path or upgrade their skills to meet the demands of a changing job market. By investing in education and training, veterans can increase their chances of finding stable, rewarding employment.

Furthermore, the VR&E program offers support for veterans who require accommodations in the workplace due to their service-connected disabilities. This may include assistive technology, specialized equipment, or modifications to the work environment to ensure equal access and opportunity. The goal is to empower veterans to overcome any barriers they may face and thrive in their chosen careers.

Veterans can access VR&E services by contacting their local VA office or by visiting the VA website. They will be assigned a vocational rehabilitation counselor who will guide them through the process and provide ongoing support. It is important for veterans and their families to be aware of this valuable resource and take advantage of the services available to them.

In conclusion, the Vocational Rehabilitation and Employment Services provided by the VA are a critical component of the comprehensive healthcare benefits available to American veterans and their families. By offering career counseling, vocational training, job placement assistance, and support for workplace accommodations, the VR&E program aims to empower veterans with service-connected disabilities to achieve their employment goals. Whether it is pursuing education, upgrading skills, or finding meaningful employment, veterans can rely on the VR&E program to provide the necessary support and resources for a successful career transition.

Entrepreneurship and Small Business Support for Veterans

Starting a small business can be a challenging endeavor, but for veterans, it can also be a pathway to success and independence. Recognizing the unique skills and experiences that veterans bring to the table, there are numerous resources and support systems available to help them navigate the world of entrepreneurship and small business ownership.

One of the key benefits of entrepreneurship for veterans is the opportunity to create their own career path. Many veterans possess valuable leadership, problem-solving, and organizational skills that are highly transferable to the business world. By starting their own business, veterans can leverage these skills and turn their passion into a profitable venture.

To support veterans in their entrepreneurial journey, there are various programs and initiatives in place. The Small Business Administration (SBA), for example, offers a range of resources specifically tailored to veterans. These include training programs, mentorship opportunities, and financial assistance in the form of loans and grants.

In addition to the SBA, there are numerous nonprofit organizations dedicated to supporting veteran-owned businesses. These organizations provide not only financial resources but also mentorship, networking opportunities, and access to markets and contracts specifically earmarked for veteran-owned businesses.

Furthermore, many states and local communities have established programs to encourage and support veteran entrepreneurship. These programs may offer tax incentives, access to business incubators, and specialized training and counseling services.

For veterans interested in starting a small business, it is crucial to take advantage of these resources and support systems. Conducting thorough research, attending workshops and training sessions, and seeking guidance from mentors can greatly increase the chances of success.

Moreover, veterans should also explore opportunities for certification as a service-disabled veteran-owned small business (SDVOSB) or veteran-owned small business (VOSB). These certifications can provide access to government contracts and procurement opportunities that are exclusively set aside for veteran-owned businesses.

In conclusion, entrepreneurship and small business ownership offer veterans a unique avenue for personal and professional growth. By taking advantage of the resources and support systems available, veterans can transition into successful business owners and contribute to the economy while creating fulfilling careers for themselves.

Professional Development and Continuing Education Opportunities

As veterans and their families navigate the complex world of healthcare benefits, it is essential to recognize the importance of ongoing education and professional development. In this subchapter, we will explore the various opportunities available to veterans and their families to enhance their skills, expand their knowledge, and advance their careers.

Continuing education is crucial for staying current with the latest advancements in healthcare. Many organizations offer specialized training programs, workshops, and conferences specifically designed for veterans. These events cover a wide range of topics, including new treatment modalities, technological advancements, and best practices in patient care. By taking advantage of these opportunities, veterans can not only enhance their knowledge but also improve the quality of care they provide to their fellow veterans.

In addition to healthcare-specific education, veterans should also explore educational benefits available to them. The Post-9/11 GI Bill offers valuable educational assistance, including tuition and housing allowances, to veterans pursuing higher education or vocational training. This benefit can be used to obtain degrees or certifications in various healthcare fields, such as nursing, medical assisting, or healthcare administration. Taking advantage of these educational benefits can significantly enhance veterans' career prospects and open doors to new opportunities in the healthcare industry.

Furthermore, veterans and their families should consider professional development programs offered by government agencies, non-profit organizations, and private companies. These programs provide veterans with valuable skills training, resume building, and networking opportunities. They can also help veterans transition into civilian careers by offering job placement services and connecting them with employers who value the unique skills and experiences veterans bring to the table.

Continuing education and professional development opportunities can also contribute to the financial well-being of veterans and their families. By acquiring new skills and certifications, veterans can enhance their earning potential and increase their chances of securing higher-paying jobs in the healthcare industry. Additionally, some educational programs offer financial assistance, scholarships, or loan forgiveness options, further easing the financial burden of pursuing further education or training.

In conclusion, professional development and continuing education opportunities are essential for veterans and their families looking to maximize their healthcare benefits. By staying current with the latest advancements in healthcare, acquiring new skills and certifications, and pursuing higher education, veterans can enhance their career prospects, improve their financial situation, and provide the best possible care to their fellow veterans. It is crucial for veterans and their families to explore the various educational and professional development programs available to them and take full advantage of the benefits they offer.

# Chapter 6: Disability Compensation Benefits for American Veterans

Understanding Disability Compensation for Veterans

Disability compensation is a crucial benefit that is available to veterans who have sustained injuries or developed medical conditions as a result of their military service. This subchapter aims to provide veterans and their families with a comprehensive understanding of disability compensation and how it can support them in their post-service lives.

The first thing to understand about disability compensation is that it is a financial benefit provided by the Department of Veterans Affairs (VA) to veterans with service-related disabilities. These disabilities can range from physical injuries, such as loss of limb or hearing impairment, to mental health conditions like post-traumatic stress disorder (PTSD) or depression.

To be eligible for disability compensation, veterans must have a current diagnosis of a disability that is directly connected to their military service. It is important to note that the disability does not have to manifest immediately after leaving the service; it can develop years later. However, it must be proven that the disability is a result of military service.

The amount of compensation a veteran receives depends on the severity of their disability, as determined by the VA. The VA uses a rating system, ranging from 0 to 100 percent, to assess the level of disability. The higher the rating, the more compensation the veteran is eligible to receive.

In addition to monthly compensation, veterans with severe disabilities may also be eligible for additional benefits, such as grants for adaptive equipment or assistance with home modifications to accommodate their disability.

Navigating the complex process of applying for disability compensation can be challenging, but there is assistance available. Veterans and their families can seek guidance from accredited service organizations, such as the Disabled American Veterans (DAV) or the American Legion, who can provide expert advice and help with the application process.

Understanding disability compensation is essential for veterans and their families to ensure they receive the support they deserve. This benefit can provide financial stability, access to medical care, and assistance with daily living for veterans with service-related disabilities. By exploring the resources available and seeking assistance when needed, veterans can make the most of this vital benefit and improve their quality of life after their honorable service to our country.

Service-Connected Disabilities and Compensation Claims

One of the most important aspects of healthcare benefits for American veterans is the recognition and compensation for service-connected disabilities. This subchapter will provide a comprehensive guide to understanding service-connected disabilities and how to file compensation claims.

Service-connected disabilities are injuries, illnesses, or disabilities that were incurred or aggravated during military service. These disabilities can be physical, such as loss of limb or hearing, or mental, such as post-traumatic stress disorder (PTSD) or traumatic brain injury (TBI). It is crucial for veterans and their families to understand that these disabilities are a result of their dedicated service to the country and that they are entitled to compensation.

To file a compensation claim, veterans need to provide evidence that their disability is connected to their military service. This can include medical records, service records, and statements from medical professionals. It is recommended to seek assistance from a Veterans Service Officer (VSO) or a qualified attorney who can guide you through the process and ensure that all necessary documentation is submitted.

The compensation amount for service-connected disabilities varies depending on the severity of the disability. The Department of Veterans Affairs (VA) uses a rating system to determine the level of disability and provides compensation accordingly. Veterans and their families should be aware of the different rating percentages and how they affect the compensation amount.

In addition to compensation, veterans with service-connected disabilities may also be eligible for other benefits. These benefits can include healthcare coverage, vocational rehabilitation, adaptive housing grants, and assistive devices. It is essential to explore all the available benefits to ensure that veterans and their families receive the support they need.

Filing a compensation claim for service-connected disabilities can be a complex process. However, it is crucial for veterans and their families to understand their rights and seek the benefits they deserve. By educating themselves about service-connected disabilities and compensation claims, veterans can navigate the system more effectively and receive the support they need to live fulfilling lives after their military service.

This subchapter will provide detailed information on the documentation required for compensation claims, the rating system used by the VA, and the additional benefits available to veterans with service-connected disabilities. By understanding this information, veterans and their families can make informed decisions and access the healthcare benefits they deserve.

Overall, this subchapter aims to empower veterans and their families by providing them with the knowledge and resources necessary to navigate the compensation claims process successfully and access the benefits they are entitled to.

VA Disability Rating System and Compensation Rates

Title: VA Disability Rating System and Compensation Rates

Introduction:

In this subchapter, we will delve into the VA Disability Rating System and Compensation Rates, which play a crucial role in ensuring that American veterans and their families receive the appropriate benefits and support they deserve. Understanding this system is essential for maximizing the available healthcare benefits, educational assistance, housing benefits, employment opportunities, and much more.

VA Disability Rating System:

The VA Disability Rating System evaluates the severity and impact of service-connected disabilities, assigning a rating percentage from 0 to 100%. This rating represents the level of impairment and determines the compensation and other benefits veterans are eligible for. The system considers both physical and mental conditions, ensuring a comprehensive assessment of each individual's unique circumstances.

Compensation Rates:

Compensation rates vary based on the assigned disability rating percentage. The VA uses a complex formula that takes into account the veteran's marital status, number of dependents, and overall disability rating. The compensation received aims to provide financial assistance to veterans and their families, compensating for the disabilities incurred during their service to the nation.

Understanding the Benefits:

The compensation received through the VA Disability Rating System can significantly impact various aspects of veterans' lives. It is important for veterans and their families to comprehend the potential benefits these rates can unlock across different areas:

1. Healthcare benefits: Access to comprehensive medical care, including specialized treatments for service-connected disabilities.

2. Educational benefits: Financial assistance for pursuing higher education, vocational training, or skill development.

3. Housing benefits: Assistance with home loans, mortgage programs, adaptive housing grants, and housing allowances.

4. Employment and career benefits: Priority consideration for federal job opportunities, vocational rehabilitation, and job training programs.

5. Financial assistance benefits: Additional financial support through grants, pensions, and financial counseling services.

6. Mental health and counseling benefits: Access to counseling services, support groups, and mental health treatments.

7. Burial and memorial benefits: Assistance with funeral expenses, burial in national cemeteries, and memorial markers.

8. Home loan and mortgage benefits: Special loan programs and refinancing options for purchasing, building, or renovating homes.

9. Small business and entrepreneurship benefits: Resources, loans, and mentorship programs to support veteran-owned small businesses.

Conclusion:

The VA Disability Rating System and Compensation Rates are an integral part of ensuring veterans receive the support they deserve. By understanding these systems, veterans and their families can access the wide range of benefits available to them, enhancing their quality of life, financial security, and overall well-being.

Benefits for Specific Disabilities and Conditions

One of the most significant aspects of healthcare benefits for American veterans is the availability of specific benefits tailored to address disabilities and conditions that veterans may have acquired during their service. These benefits aim to provide comprehensive support and improve the quality of life for veterans and their families. In this subchapter, we will explore the various benefits available for specific disabilities and conditions, ensuring that veterans can access the care and assistance they need.

For veterans with physical disabilities, there are numerous benefits available to enhance mobility and independence. These include prosthetic devices, home modifications, and adaptive equipment such as wheelchairs or mobility scooters. Additionally, veterans with visual impairments can receive assistance through vision rehabilitation services and guide dogs, promoting increased autonomy and safety.

Veterans suffering from mental health conditions, such as post-traumatic stress disorder (PTSD) or depression, can access a range of specialized benefits. Mental health and counseling benefits provide therapy, counseling, and medication management to address these conditions effectively. Additionally, support groups and peer-to-peer programs are available to facilitate connection and understanding among veterans facing similar challenges.

For veterans with traumatic brain injuries (TBI) or other cognitive impairments, there are specialized benefits designed to support their unique needs. These benefits include cognitive rehabilitation, assistive technology devices, and access to memory clinics. By addressing cognitive impairments, veterans can regain cognitive abilities and improve their overall quality of life.

The Department of Veterans Affairs (VA) also provides benefits for veterans with specific conditions such as Agent Orange exposure, Gulf War Syndrome, and radiation exposure. These benefits encompass specialized healthcare, compensation for disabilities related to these conditions, and access to important resources and information.

In addition to healthcare benefits, educational assistance is available for veterans with disabilities. The VA offers vocational rehabilitation programs that provide career counseling, education, and training to help veterans reintegrate into the workforce successfully. This support ensures that veterans with disabilities can achieve their educational and career goals.

It is crucial for veterans and their families to be aware of the various benefits available for specific disabilities and conditions. By accessing these benefits, veterans can receive the necessary care and support to manage their disabilities effectively and enhance their overall well-being. The comprehensive range of benefits ensures that veterans are not only honored for their service but also provided with the resources they need to thrive in civilian life.

Appeals Process for Disability Compensation Claims

When it comes to disability compensation claims, the road to obtaining the benefits you deserve can be a challenging one. However, it is important to remember that you have the right to appeal any decision made by the Department of Veterans Affairs (VA) regarding your claim. Understanding the appeals process is crucial in ensuring that you receive the healthcare benefits you are entitled to as an American veteran.

The first step in the appeals process is to file a Notice of Disagreement (NOD) within one year of receiving the decision you wish to appeal. This notifies the VA that you disagree with their decision and want to move forward with the appeal. It is important to provide any new evidence or information that supports your claim at this stage.

After filing the NOD, your claim will be reviewed by a Decision Review Officer (DRO) who will reconsider the decision made by the VA. This review can include a formal hearing, where you have the opportunity to present your case in person. It is essential to prepare thoroughly for this hearing and gather any relevant documentation that supports your claim.

If you are still dissatisfied with the decision made by the DRO, you can take your appeal to the Board of Veterans' Appeals (BVA). At this stage, a Veterans Law Judge will review your case and make a final decision. The BVA has the authority to grant, deny, or remand your claim back to the VA for further review.

If you disagree with the decision made by the BVA, you can further appeal to the U.S. Court of Appeals for Veterans Claims (CAVC). This court is independent of the VA and has the authority to review decisions made by the BVA. It is important to note that appealing to the CAVC requires legal representation, and it is advisable to seek assistance from a veterans' service organization or an accredited attorney.

Navigating the appeals process can be complex and time-consuming, but it is essential to persist in pursuing the benefits you deserve. Remember that you are not alone in this journey – there are numerous resources available to help you understand and navigate the appeals process. Veterans' service organizations, such as the Disabled American Veterans (DAV) and the Veterans of Foreign Wars (VFW), can provide valuable guidance and support.

In conclusion, the appeals process for disability compensation claims is an important avenue for veterans and their families to receive the healthcare benefits they are entitled to. By understanding the steps involved and seeking assistance when needed, you can navigate the process with confidence and increase your chances of a successful outcome.

Special Monthly Compensation and Benefits for Dependents

Special Monthly Compensation (SMC) and Benefits for Dependents

As a veteran, you have made incredible sacrifices for your country and deserve to receive the highest level of care and support. One important aspect of this support is ensuring that your dependents are also taken care of. The Department of Veterans Affairs (VA) offers a range of special monthly compensation (SMC) and benefits for dependents to provide financial assistance and other resources to help meet their needs.

SMC for dependents is an additional monetary benefit that can be provided to veterans who have a service-connected disability rated at 30% or higher. This compensation is designed to recognize the increased level of care and assistance required for veterans with dependents. The amount of SMC varies depending on the number and type of dependents, as well as the severity of the veteran's disability.

In addition to financial compensation, the VA also offers a range of benefits to support the healthcare, education, housing, employment, and career needs of dependents. Healthcare benefits for dependents include access to comprehensive medical care, including preventive services, mental health care, and prescription medications. Educational benefits for dependents can help cover the costs of tuition, books, and supplies for college, vocational training, and other educational programs.

Housing benefits for dependents include assistance with home loans and mortgage programs, as well as grants for home modifications to accommodate disabilities. Employment and career benefits for dependents include job training, vocational rehabilitation, and assistance with job placement. The VA also provides disability compensation benefits to dependents in case of the veteran's death or permanent and total disability.

Financial assistance benefits for dependents can help with essential living expenses, such as housing, utilities, and transportation. Mental health and counseling benefits are available to dependents to ensure they receive the support they need to cope with the challenges that may arise from the veteran's service-related disabilities. Burial and memorial benefits provide assistance with funeral expenses, burial plots, and headstones for eligible dependents.

To access these benefits, dependents should contact their local VA office or visit the VA website for more information and guidance. The VA is committed to supporting veterans and their families in every possible way, and the range of benefits available for dependents is a testament to this commitment.

In conclusion, special monthly compensation and benefits for dependents are essential resources that ensure the well-being and care of veterans' families. From healthcare and education to housing and employment, the VA provides a comprehensive range of support services to help dependents thrive. Take advantage of these benefits and ensure that your loved ones receive the assistance they deserve.

# Chapter 7: Financial Assistance Benefits for American Veterans

Retirement and Pension Programs for Veterans

As veterans transition from their military service to civilian life, it is crucial for them and their families to be aware of the various retirement and pension programs available to them. These programs aim to provide financial stability and security for veterans throughout their retirement years. In this subchapter, we will explore the different retirement and pension programs designed specifically for American veterans.

One of the primary retirement programs available to veterans is the Veterans Pension program. This program offers monthly payments to veterans who have served during wartime and meet certain income and asset requirements. The Veterans Pension program provides additional financial support to veterans who are disabled or over the age of 65, ensuring they have a comfortable retirement.

Another retirement program that veterans can benefit from is the Survivor Benefit Plan (SBP). The SBP is a program that provides a monthly annuity to eligible survivors of deceased veterans. This annuity ensures that the surviving spouse or dependent children continue to receive financial support after the veteran's passing. The SBP offers peace of mind and financial stability to the families of veterans.

In addition to retirement programs, there are various pension programs available to veterans. The most notable one is the Department of Veterans Affairs (VA) Disability Pension, which provides financial assistance to veterans with disabilities that are not service-connected.

This pension program ensures that veterans with disabilities have access to financial resources to support their needs.

It is important for veterans and their families to understand the eligibility criteria and application process for these retirement and pension programs. They should consult with a Veterans Service Officer or reach out to the VA for guidance and assistance. By taking advantage of these programs, veterans can secure their financial future and enjoy a well-deserved retirement.

In conclusion, retirement and pension programs for veterans play a vital role in ensuring their financial stability and security. These programs provide monthly payments, annuities, and financial assistance to veterans and their families, offering peace of mind throughout their retirement years. By exploring and understanding the various retirement and pension programs available, veterans can make informed decisions and access the benefits they have earned through their honorable service to our nation.

Financial Counseling and Debt Management Services

In this subchapter, we will explore the importance of financial counseling and debt management services for American veterans and their families. While veterans have access to numerous benefits and resources, it is crucial to understand the significance of proper financial management to ensure long-term stability and well-being.

Financial counseling services provide expert guidance and support in managing personal finances, budgeting, and debt management. These services can help veterans and their families develop a comprehensive financial plan tailored to their unique needs and goals. By working with a financial counselor, veterans can gain a better understanding of their financial situation, learn strategies to reduce debt, and create a budget that aligns with their income and expenses.

Debt management services are particularly beneficial for veterans facing financial hardships or struggling with excessive debt. These services offer assistance in negotiating with creditors, creating manageable repayment plans, and providing strategies to avoid future debt. By seeking debt management services, veterans can alleviate the stress and burden of debt, allowing them to focus on other aspects of their lives, such as healthcare, education, and housing.

Proper financial management is essential for veterans to make the most of their healthcare benefits. By effectively managing their finances, veterans can afford necessary medical treatments, medications, and preventive care. Financial counseling can help veterans navigate complex healthcare systems, understand insurance options, and minimize out-of-pocket expenses.

Moreover, financial counseling plays a crucial role in maximizing educational benefits for veterans. By creating a sound financial plan, veterans can determine the feasibility of pursuing higher education, access educational grants and scholarships, and make informed decisions regarding student loans. Financial counselors can provide guidance on minimizing educational expenses, managing student loan debt, and identifying career pathways that align with veterans' skills and interests.

Additionally, financial counseling and debt management services can assist veterans in accessing housing benefits, employment and career benefits, disability compensation benefits, mental health and counseling benefits, burial and memorial benefits, home loan and mortgage benefits, as well as small business and entrepreneurship benefits. Proper financial management enhances veterans' ability to make informed decisions, seize opportunities, and secure a stable future for themselves and their families.

By availing themselves of financial counseling and debt management services, veterans can gain the necessary tools and knowledge to achieve financial stability, make sound financial decisions, and optimize the benefits available to them. The resources and support provided by these services are invaluable in helping veterans and their families navigate the complex world of personal finance and create a solid foundation for their future.

Financial Assistance for Homeless and At-Risk Veterans

In times of crisis, it is crucial for veterans and their families to have access to the necessary financial assistance to ensure their well-being and stability. For those who find themselves homeless or at risk of homelessness, various programs and resources are available to help veterans regain their footing and secure a brighter future.

One of the primary sources of financial aid for homeless and at-risk veterans is the Department of Veterans Affairs (VA). The VA offers a range of programs and services designed specifically to address housing needs. These programs include the Supportive Services for Veteran Families (SSVF) program, which provides short-term financial assistance for rental payments, utility bills, and security deposits. Additionally, the VA's Grant and Per Diem (GPD) program offers transitional housing and supportive services to homeless veterans.

In addition to the VA's programs, there are numerous non-profit organizations and community-based initiatives dedicated to assisting homeless and at-risk veterans. These organizations often provide emergency financial assistance for housing, transportation, and other immediate needs. They may also offer case management services to help veterans navigate the complex process of finding stable housing and accessing necessary resources.

Furthermore, it is important for veterans and their families to be aware of the state and local resources available to them. Many states offer specific programs and benefits aimed at addressing homelessness among veterans. These programs may include rental assistance, job training, and supportive services tailored to the unique needs of veterans.

When seeking financial assistance, veterans and their families should also consider exploring educational and employment benefits. By taking advantage of programs such as the GI Bill and the Vocational Rehabilitation and Employment (VR&E) program, veterans can enhance their skills and increase their employability, ultimately contributing to their long-term financial stability.

In conclusion, financial assistance for homeless and at-risk veterans is a critical component of ensuring their well-being and successful reintegration into society. By leveraging the resources provided by the VA, non-profit organizations, and state and local agencies, veterans and their families can access the support they need to secure stable housing, obtain employment, and build a brighter future. It is essential for veterans and their families to be informed about the various financial assistance programs available to them and to seek help when needed. Remember, you are not alone – there is support available to help you overcome any financial challenges you may face.

Emergency Financial Assistance Programs for Veterans

In times of financial crisis, veterans and their families may face unexpected expenses or find themselves struggling to make ends meet. Fortunately, there are several emergency financial assistance programs available to provide support and relief during difficult times. This subchapter aims to provide a comprehensive guide to these programs, ensuring that veterans and their families are aware of the resources available to them.

One notable program is the Veterans Emergency Fund, which offers immediate financial aid to veterans facing unforeseen emergencies such as eviction, utility shut-offs, or medical emergencies. This fund provides short-term assistance to help veterans stabilize their situation and prevent further hardship. Additionally, there are various charitable organizations, such as the American Legion or Veterans of Foreign Wars, that offer emergency financial assistance to veterans in need.

Another avenue for emergency financial assistance is the Department of Veterans Affairs (VA). The VA provides several programs tailored to meet the unique needs of veterans and their families. For instance, the VA's Homeless Veterans Program offers support and financial assistance to veterans at risk of homelessness, including emergency housing, rental assistance, and case management services.

Furthermore, veterans who are struggling with medical bills can turn to the VA's Medical Care Hardship Program. This program offers financial relief to veterans who are unable to pay their medical expenses, ensuring they receive the care they need without incurring excessive debt.

In addition to these specific programs, veterans can also explore resources available within their local community. Many states and municipalities offer emergency financial assistance programs specifically designed for veterans and their families. These programs may provide assistance with rent, utilities, food, or other essential needs.

It is crucial for veterans and their families to be aware of these emergency financial assistance programs and to seek help when needed. Financial difficulties should not hinder veterans from accessing the support and benefits they have earned through their service to our nation. By understanding and utilizing these resources, veterans can overcome financial challenges and focus on building a stable and prosperous future.

Remember, you are not alone. There are numerous organizations, government programs, and community resources dedicated to supporting veterans and their families in times of need. Reach out, ask for help, and let the network of support designed for you be there when you need it most.

Tax Benefits and Exemptions for Veterans

As a veteran, you have made countless sacrifices to protect and serve our country. In recognition of your service, the government offers a range of tax benefits and exemptions to help ease your financial burden. Understanding these benefits can make a significant difference in your financial planning and overall well-being. In this subchapter, we will explore the various tax benefits and exemptions available to veterans and their families.

One of the most significant tax benefits for veterans is the Disability Compensation. If you have a service-connected disability, you may be eligible for tax-free monthly compensation. This compensation is not subject to federal income tax, ensuring that you receive the full amount to support your needs.

In addition to disability compensation, veterans may also qualify for exemptions on property taxes. Many states provide property tax breaks for disabled veterans, reducing the financial strain of homeownership. These exemptions can vary depending on your state, so it is crucial to research the specific criteria and application process in your area.

Another tax benefit for veterans is the VA Pension, a needs-based program that provides additional income for wartime veterans who have limited income and are over 65 years of age or permanently disabled. This pension is also tax-free, ensuring that you receive the maximum benefit to support your daily living expenses.

Furthermore, veterans who are starting or expanding small businesses may be eligible for tax incentives. The government offers various tax credits and deductions to encourage veteran entrepreneurship and job creation. These benefits can include deductions for start-up expenses, tax credits for hiring veterans, and preferential treatment in government contracting.

It is worth noting that tax benefits and exemptions can be complex, and eligibility criteria may vary depending on your circumstances. Therefore, it is highly recommended to consult with a tax professional or veterans' service organization to ensure you are taking full advantage of the available benefits.

In conclusion, as a veteran, you are entitled to a range of tax benefits and exemptions to support your financial well-being. From disability compensation to property tax exemptions and small business incentives, these benefits aim to recognize your service and alleviate any financial burdens you may face. Taking advantage of these benefits can help you build a stronger financial future for yourself and your family.

Insurance and Legal Assistance Programs for Veterans

In addition to the numerous healthcare, educational, housing, employment, disability compensation, financial assistance, mental health, counseling, burial and memorial, home loan and mortgage, small business, and entrepreneurship benefits available to American veterans, there are also specialized insurance and legal assistance programs specifically designed to support veterans and their families. These programs aim to provide financial protection and legal guidance to ensure veterans have the necessary resources to navigate life after military service.

One of the key insurance programs available to veterans is the Servicemembers' Group Life Insurance (SGLI). SGLI provides low-cost life insurance coverage to eligible veterans and service members. It offers coverage up to $400,000 and can be extended for up to two years following separation from service. Additionally, veterans who are totally disabled due to a service-connected injury may qualify for the Veterans' Mortgage Life Insurance (VMLI) program, which helps to pay off the remaining mortgage balance on their home in the event of their death.

Legal assistance programs are also crucial for veterans and their families, as they provide guidance and support in navigating complex legal matters. The U.S. Department of Veterans Affairs (VA) offers free legal services through the Veterans Justice Outreach (VJO) program. This program provides assistance with a range of legal issues, including housing and eviction matters, family law, and issues related to employment and benefits.

Furthermore, veterans can also benefit from the assistance of Veterans Service Organizations (VSOs) that provide legal aid. VSOs play a vital role in advocating for veterans' rights and can help veterans access legal representation, file claims for disability benefits, and address other legal concerns. These organizations often have extensive experience working with veterans and can provide valuable guidance throughout the legal process.

It is important for veterans and their families to be aware of the insurance and legal assistance programs available to them. These programs can provide financial protection and legal support in times of need, ensuring that veterans can access the benefits and services they deserve. By utilizing these resources, veterans can navigate the complexities of post-military life with confidence, knowing that they have the necessary support networks in place.

# Chapter 8: Mental Health and Counseling Benefits for American Veterans

Mental Health Services for Veterans

When it comes to the well-being of our veterans, mental health is an essential aspect that must not be overlooked. Serving in the armed forces can take a significant toll on one's mental health, and it is crucial for veterans and their families to be aware of the various mental health services available to them.

Mental health services for veterans encompass a range of resources and support systems designed to address the unique challenges faced by those who have served in the military. These services aim to provide both preventive and therapeutic interventions to promote mental wellness and help veterans lead fulfilling lives.

One of the key mental health benefits available to veterans is counseling. The Department of Veterans Affairs (VA) offers counseling services through various programs, such as the Vet Center Program and the Veterans Crisis Line. These programs provide confidential counseling and support to veterans and their families, helping them navigate challenges such as post-traumatic stress disorder (PTSD), depression, anxiety, and substance abuse.

In addition to counseling, the VA also provides access to specialized mental health treatment. This includes programs tailored to address the unique needs of veterans, such as the Women Veterans Program, which offers gender-specific mental health care, and the Military Sexual Trauma Support Program, which provides assistance to veterans who have experienced sexual assault or harassment during their service.

Furthermore, the VA has established partnerships with community-based organizations to ensure veterans have access to a wide range of mental health services. These partnerships help connect veterans to local resources, support groups, and therapy options, allowing them to receive care close to home.

It is important for veterans and their families to be proactive in seeking mental health services. By reaching out to the VA, veterans can undergo comprehensive mental health assessments and receive personalized treatment plans. These plans may include a combination of therapy, medication, and other interventions to address specific mental health concerns.

In conclusion, mental health services for veterans play a vital role in ensuring their overall well-being. By taking advantage of the counseling, specialized treatment programs, and community partnerships offered by the VA, veterans and their families can receive the support they need to address mental health challenges effectively. It is essential for veterans to be aware of these resources and to reach out for assistance when necessary, as mental health is a crucial aspect of their overall healthcare benefits.

PTSD and Trauma-related Care for Veterans

When it comes to healthcare benefits for American veterans, it is crucial to address the specific needs of those who have experienced trauma during their service. Post-Traumatic Stress Disorder (PTSD) is a common condition that affects many veterans, and it is essential to provide them with the necessary care and support.

PTSD is a mental health disorder that can develop after experiencing a traumatic event. For veterans, this trauma may result from combat, witnessing violence, or other life-threatening situations. The symptoms of PTSD can be debilitating, including flashbacks, nightmares, anxiety, and emotional distress.

Fortunately, there are dedicated healthcare benefits available to veterans and their families to address PTSD and trauma-related care. These benefits provide access to specialized treatment options, such as counseling, therapy, and medication, all aimed at helping veterans manage their symptoms and improve their overall well-being.

The Department of Veterans Affairs (VA) plays a crucial role in providing mental health and counseling benefits for veterans. They have established numerous programs and initiatives to ensure that veterans receive the care they deserve. These programs aim to reduce the stigma surrounding mental health issues and encourage veterans to seek help.

In addition to counseling and therapy, the VA also offers support groups and peer-to-peer programs. These resources allow veterans to connect with others who have experienced similar traumas, providing a sense of community and understanding. Family members of veterans may also benefit from support services to help them navigate the challenges of living with a loved one who has PTSD.

It is important for veterans and their families to be aware of the various healthcare benefits available to them. By understanding their options, they can access the necessary care and support to manage PTSD and trauma-related issues effectively.

In conclusion, PTSD and trauma-related care are critical components of healthcare benefits for American veterans. Through specialized treatment options, counseling, and support programs, veterans can receive the care they need to manage their symptoms and improve their overall well-being. By taking advantage of these benefits, veterans and their families can find the support and resources necessary to live fulfilling lives after their service.

Substance Abuse and Addiction Treatment for Veterans

For veterans and their families, understanding the available healthcare benefits is crucial in order to receive the comprehensive care they deserve. One important aspect of healthcare benefits for American veterans is substance abuse and addiction treatment. This subchapter aims to provide veterans and their families with a comprehensive guide on available resources and support for overcoming substance abuse and addiction.

Veterans often face unique challenges that can contribute to substance abuse and addiction. The stressors of military service, exposure to traumatic events, and the transition back to civilian life can all contribute to the development of substance abuse issues. Recognizing the signs and seeking help is the first step towards recovery.

The Department of Veterans Affairs (VA) provides a range of substance abuse and addiction treatment options for veterans. These include both inpatient and outpatient programs, as well as specialized services tailored to the needs of veterans. Treatment options may include detoxification, counseling, medication-assisted therapy, and support groups.

In addition to the VA, veterans may also benefit from community-based organizations and support groups that provide substance abuse and addiction treatment. These organizations can offer additional resources, peer support, and counseling services specifically designed for veterans and their families.

It is important to note that veterans may also be eligible for educational benefits, housing benefits, employment and career benefits, disability compensation benefits, financial assistance benefits, mental health and counseling benefits, burial and memorial benefits, home loan and mortgage benefits, as well as small business and entrepreneurship benefits. All these benefits can contribute to the overall well-being of veterans and their families.

Overcoming substance abuse and addiction is a challenging journey, but with the right support, it is possible. By taking advantage of the healthcare benefits available specifically for veterans, individuals can access the necessary resources and treatment options to reclaim their lives and reintegrate into society.

In conclusion, substance abuse and addiction treatment for veterans is a vital component of healthcare benefits. By seeking help and utilizing the available resources, veterans can overcome substance abuse issues and rebuild their lives. It is crucial for veterans and their families to be aware of the support and treatment options that are available to them through the VA and community organizations. This subchapter serves as a comprehensive guide for veterans and their families, providing them with the knowledge and tools they need to address substance abuse and addiction effectively.

Support for Military Sexual Trauma Survivors

Military Sexual Trauma (MST) is a pervasive issue that affects many service members, and it is crucial for veterans and their families to understand the support available to survivors. This subchapter aims to provide comprehensive information on the resources and benefits available to MST survivors, ensuring they receive the care they deserve.

The Department of Veterans Affairs (VA) recognizes the significance of MST and has established specialized programs to support survivors. The VA offers a range of services focused on assisting MST survivors in their physical, emotional, and mental recovery. These services include counseling, medical treatment, and support groups tailored specifically for MST survivors.

Counseling is a vital component of healing for MST survivors. The VA provides individual and group therapy sessions, allowing survivors to address their trauma in a safe and supportive environment. Additionally, the VA has trained professionals who specialize in treating Military Sexual Trauma, ensuring survivors receive the best possible care.

Medical treatment is also available to MST survivors. The VA offers comprehensive healthcare services, including specialized care for physical injuries resulting from MST. Survivors can access medical professionals who are experienced in addressing the unique challenges faced by MST survivors, ensuring their physical well-being is prioritized.

Furthermore, the VA recognizes the importance of raising awareness about MST and preventing future incidents. The VA actively promotes education and outreach programs to inform service members and their families about the signs of MST and the resources available to survivors. By increasing awareness, the VA aims to create a supportive environment that encourages survivors to seek help and promotes a culture of respect within the military community.

In addition to the VA's support, various nonprofit organizations and advocacy groups focus specifically on MST survivors. These organizations provide additional resources, support, and legal assistance for survivors seeking justice.

It is important for veterans and their families to be aware of the support available to MST survivors. By accessing these resources, survivors can begin their healing journey and regain control of their lives. The VA and other organizations are dedicated to ensuring that MST survivors receive the care they need and deserve, and no survivor should hesitate to seek assistance. Together, we can create a safer and more supportive environment for all veterans and their families.

Suicide Prevention and Crisis Intervention Services

In times of crisis and overwhelming emotions, it is crucial for veterans and their families to know that they are never alone. The journey of transitioning from military to civilian life can be challenging, and it's not uncommon for individuals to face mental health issues such as depression, anxiety, and post-traumatic stress disorder (PTSD). Recognizing the importance of mental well-being, the Department of Veterans Affairs (VA) has established a range of suicide prevention and crisis intervention services to provide the necessary support and care.

One of the key initiatives in suicide prevention is the Veterans Crisis Line, which offers free, confidential support 24/7 to veterans, service members, and their families. By calling, texting, or chatting online, individuals can connect with trained professionals who understand the unique challenges faced by veterans. These compassionate responders can provide immediate assistance, offer emotional support, and even facilitate connections to local VA facilities or community resources.

Additionally, the VA has implemented the Suicide Prevention Coordinators (SPCs) program across all VA medical centers. These dedicated professionals serve as points of contact to help veterans navigate the available services and resources. SPCs work closely with mental health providers, social workers, and community organizations to ensure comprehensive care and support for those in crisis.

Recognizing the importance of early intervention, the VA has also developed programs like the Veterans Crisis Line's "Be There" campaign. This initiative aims to educate families, friends, and communities on how to recognize warning signs and provide support to veterans in need. By fostering a network of care, the VA strives to create a safety net that can help prevent crises and promote well-being.

It is important for veterans and their families to be aware of the various mental health and counseling benefits available to them. These services encompass individual therapy, group counseling, marriage and family counseling, and even programs specifically designed for combat veterans or survivors of military sexual trauma. By accessing these resources, veterans can find solace, develop coping strategies, and regain control of their lives.

In conclusion, suicide prevention and crisis intervention services are invaluable resources for veterans and their families. The VA's commitment to mental health support ensures that no one has to face their struggles alone. By utilizing these services, veterans can find the help they need to overcome challenges, heal, and thrive in civilian life. Remember, there is always hope and support available to you.

Family and Relationship Counseling for Veterans

One of the often overlooked aspects of healthcare benefits for American veterans is family and relationship counseling. Serving in the military can take a toll on veterans and their families, and it is essential to address the unique challenges they may face. This subchapter explores the importance of family and relationship counseling for veterans and how it can positively impact their overall well-being.

Veterans and their families often experience a range of difficulties, including communication breakdowns, post-traumatic stress disorder (PTSD), depression, anxiety, and substance abuse. These issues can strain relationships and have a significant impact on the veteran's mental health. Family and relationship counseling can provide a safe space for veterans and their families to address these challenges and work towards healing and growth.

One of the primary benefits of family and relationship counseling is improved communication. Many veterans struggle to express their emotions or may feel misunderstood by their loved ones. Counseling sessions can help facilitate open and honest communication, allowing family members to gain a better understanding of each other's experiences and perspectives. This can lead to stronger bonds and healthier relationships within the family unit.

Additionally, family and relationship counseling can help veterans and their families navigate the effects of PTSD and other mental health conditions. Therapists trained in working with military families can provide specialized interventions that address the unique challenges faced by veterans. This may include learning coping strategies, developing healthy boundaries, and resolving past traumas.

Furthermore, family and relationship counseling can also assist in addressing any financial or housing difficulties that veterans and their families may be facing. Counselors can provide guidance on accessing housing benefits, financial assistance, and other resources available to veterans. They can also help veterans and their families develop effective strategies for managing stress and maintaining a healthy work-life balance.

In conclusion, family and relationship counseling is a crucial component of healthcare benefits for American veterans. It offers support and guidance to veterans and their families, helping them navigate the challenges that arise from military service. By addressing communication breakdowns, mental health issues, and other difficulties, counseling can strengthen family bonds, improve overall well-being, and enhance the quality of life for veterans and their loved ones.

# Chapter 9: Burial and Memorial Benefits for American Veterans

Overview of Burial Benefits for Veterans

One of the significant benefits available to American veterans and their families is the comprehensive burial and memorial benefits provided by the Department of Veterans Affairs (VA). These benefits honor the service and sacrifice of veterans by ensuring they receive a dignified final resting place.

Burial benefits provided by the VA include a variety of services and allowances to help veterans and their families during this challenging time. These benefits are available to eligible veterans regardless of their position at the time of death, whether they were on active duty, reserves, or have been discharged.

First and foremost, the VA provides burial in a national cemetery for eligible veterans. This includes opening and closing of the grave, perpetual care, and the placement of a government headstone or marker. Alternatively, if the veteran chooses to be buried in a private cemetery, the VA provides a headstone or marker, as well as a burial plot allowance to cover the cost of the grave.

Another important benefit is the burial flag, which is draped over the casket or urn during the funeral service. After the funeral, the flag is folded and presented to the veteran's next of kin as a symbol of their loved one's honorable service.

Additionally, the VA offers financial assistance to cover burial and funeral expenses. This includes a burial allowance, which helps offset the costs of funeral and burial services, and a plot or interment allowance for veterans buried in a private cemetery. These allowances are designed to alleviate the financial burden on the families of veterans.

In cases where a veteran's remains are not recoverable, the VA offers memorialization in a national cemetery, such as a memorial headstone, marker, or plaque. This ensures that even if the veteran's body is not found, their memory will be honored and recognized.

It is important for veterans and their families to be aware of these burial benefits and to plan accordingly. By understanding the options available, veterans can ensure that they receive the recognition and honors they deserve for their service to our nation.

In conclusion, the VA's burial and memorial benefits are an essential part of honoring and remembering our nation's veterans. These benefits provide a final resting place, financial assistance, and symbolic recognition to veterans and their families. By taking advantage of these benefits, veterans and their loved ones can find solace in knowing that their service and sacrifice will be remembered for generations to come.

National Cemeteries and Burial Options for Veterans

When it comes to honoring the sacrifices made by our nation's veterans, the United States government has established a comprehensive system of benefits and services. One crucial aspect of this system is the provision of burial and memorial benefits for veterans. In this subchapter, we will explore the various options available to veterans and their families in terms of national cemeteries and burial options.

The Department of Veterans Affairs (VA) operates several national cemeteries across the country, specifically designed for the interment of veterans. These cemeteries offer a final resting place that reflects the dignity and respect our veterans deserve. They provide a tranquil and sacred environment for families to remember and honor their loved ones.

Veterans and their eligible dependents are entitled to burial in one of these national cemeteries at no cost to the family. This benefit includes a gravesite, opening and closing of the grave, perpetual care, a government headstone or marker, a burial flag, and a Presidential Memorial Certificate. Additionally, some cemeteries offer optional services such as military funeral honors and the opportunity to have the burial service live-streamed for those unable to attend in person.

In addition to national cemeteries, the VA also provides burial allowances or reimbursements for veterans who choose to be buried in private or state-run cemeteries. These allowances help offset some of the costs associated with burial, such as the plot, burial vault, and headstone or marker. Eligibility for these burial allowances depends on various factors, including the veteran's service-connected disability status and the circumstances of their death.

It is important for veterans and their families to be aware of these burial benefits and options. Planning for end-of-life arrangements can alleviate the burden on loved ones during an already difficult time. The VA provides resources and assistance to help veterans and their families navigate the process, ensuring they receive the benefits they are entitled to.

In conclusion, the United States government recognizes the sacrifices made by our veterans and provides comprehensive burial and memorial benefits. National cemeteries offer a dignified and sacred final resting place, while burial allowances support veterans who choose private or state-run cemeteries. By understanding these options and planning ahead, veterans and their families can ensure they receive the honors and benefits they deserve.

Funeral and Memorial Services for Veterans

Honoring the brave men and women who have served our country is a solemn duty that we hold dear. In this subchapter, we will explore the comprehensive range of funeral and memorial services available to veterans and their families, ensuring that their loved ones receive the respect and recognition they deserve.

The Department of Veterans Affairs (VA) provides a variety of benefits to assist with funeral and memorial services. First and foremost, eligible veterans are entitled to a gravesite in one of the 155 national cemeteries across the country. These hallowed grounds offer a final resting place that is beautifully maintained and perpetually cared for.

In addition to a gravesite, the VA provides a headstone or marker, as well as a burial flag to drape over the casket or accompany the urn. The headstone or marker can be personalized with the veteran's name, rank, branch of service, and other requested information, ensuring a lasting tribute to their service.

For those veterans who choose cremation, the VA offers the option of interment in a national cemetery or the scattering of ashes in designated areas. Veterans and their families can also request a Presidential Memorial Certificate, signed by the President, as a symbol of gratitude for their loved one's service.

Furthermore, the VA offers financial assistance to help cover burial and funeral costs. This includes a burial allowance, which can help offset expenses such as transportation of the remains, preparation of the body, and use of funeral home facilities. Additionally, a plot allowance may be available for veterans who choose to be buried in a private cemetery.

It is important to note that these benefits are not automatically provided. Veterans and their families must apply for them through the VA. This can be done by contacting the nearest VA regional office or by working with a funeral director who is knowledgeable about VA benefits.

In conclusion, the funeral and memorial services available to veterans are a testament to our nation's gratitude for their sacrifice. From national cemeteries to personalized headstones, the VA ensures that each veteran is honored with dignity and respect. By understanding and accessing these benefits, veterans and their families can navigate this challenging time with peace of mind, knowing that their loved ones will be remembered and celebrated for generations to come.

Headstones, Markers, and Presidential Memorial Certificates

When a beloved veteran passes away, it is important to honor their service and sacrifice with a fitting burial and memorial. The U.S. Department of Veterans Affairs (VA) provides various benefits to ensure that every veteran receives a dignified final resting place. This subchapter will explore the options available for headstones, markers, and Presidential Memorial Certificates.

One of the most significant benefits offered by the VA is the provision of a headstone or marker for eligible veterans. This includes both traditional burial options and cremation. The headstones and markers are made of durable materials such as granite or marble and bear the name, rank, and branch of service of the deceased veteran. These markers can be personalized with emblems or symbols that represent the veteran's faith or belief system.

In addition to headstones and markers, the VA also offers Presidential Memorial Certificates to honor the memory of deceased veterans. These certificates are signed by the President of the United States and express the nation's gratitude for the veteran's service. They can be framed and displayed alongside the headstone or marker as a symbol of honor and remembrance.

To apply for these benefits, veterans or their family members should contact their local VA office or funeral home. The VA provides a wide range of options for headstones and markers, allowing families to choose the style and design that best reflects the veteran's personality and service. The VA also offers assistance in coordinating the delivery and installation of the headstone or marker at the chosen burial site.

It is important to note that these benefits are available to all eligible veterans, regardless of their financial situation. The VA is committed to ensuring that every veteran receives a proper burial and memorial, regardless of their circumstances.

In conclusion, headstones, markers, and Presidential Memorial Certificates are important components of honoring the memory and service of American veterans. The VA provides these benefits to ensure that every veteran receives a dignified final resting place. By taking advantage of these options, veterans and their families can commemorate their loved one's service and sacrifice for generations to come.

Burial Flags and Honor Guards for Veterans

One of the most solemn and respectful ways our nation honors its veterans is through the provision of burial flags and honor guards. These symbols of honor and gratitude serve as a final tribute to those who have selflessly served our country, ensuring they are laid to rest with the dignity and respect they deserve.

Burial flags hold great significance in our military traditions. These flags are provided to the families of deceased veterans as a token of appreciation for their loved one's service. The burial flag is meticulously folded by a ceremonial honor guard and presented to the next of kin during the funeral service. This flag, with its thirteen folds representing the original thirteen colonies, serves as a powerful reminder of the sacrifice and dedication of our nation's veterans.

Furthermore, honor guards play a vital role in memorial services for veterans. Composed of uniformed service members, honor guards render military honors at funerals, ensuring that each veteran receives a proper farewell. These honors may include the playing of Taps, the firing of a rifle salute, and the folding and presentation of the burial flag. The precision and reverence displayed by honor guards pay tribute to the veteran's service and provide comfort to their grieving families.

For veterans and their families, it is essential to be aware of the burial and memorial benefits available to them. The Department of Veterans Affairs (VA) provides these benefits to ensure that every veteran receives a dignified final tribute. To qualify, veterans must have received an honorable discharge, and in some cases, served during specific wartime periods. Eligible veterans are entitled to a burial flag, as well as military funeral honors, including an honor guard.

Additionally, veterans may be eligible for burial in a VA national cemetery. These cemeteries, located throughout the country, offer a final resting place that is both beautiful and hallowed. In addition to the grave site, veterans buried in a VA national cemetery receive perpetual care, including the maintenance of the grounds and the provision of a government-furnished headstone or marker.

In conclusion, burial flags and honor guards hold immense significance for veterans and their families. These symbols of honor and respect ensure that those who have served our country receive a dignified farewell. It is crucial for veterans and their families to be aware of the burial and memorial benefits available to them, including the provision of a burial flag and the opportunity for military funeral honors. By understanding and utilizing these benefits, we can pay tribute to our veterans and ensure their sacrifices are never forgotten.

Survivor Benefits and Support for Families

Losing a loved one who served in the military can be a difficult and overwhelming experience. In recognition of the sacrifices made by veterans and their families, the government provides survivor benefits and support to help ease the financial, emotional, and practical burdens during this challenging time.

Financial assistance is available through survivor benefits, which can include Dependency and Indemnity Compensation (DIC). DIC provides a monthly payment to the surviving spouse, children, or dependent parents of a deceased veteran. This benefit aims to replace the income lost due to the veteran's death and ensure the family's financial stability. Additionally, there may be additional benefits for survivors, such as aid and attendance allowances for spouses or children with disabilities.

Support for families extends beyond financial assistance. Counseling and mental health services are available to help survivors cope with grief and loss. These services are often offered through the Department of Veterans Affairs (VA) and can provide a safe and supportive environment for individuals to heal and rebuild their lives.

Burial and memorial benefits are another crucial aspect of survivor support. The VA offers various benefits, including a burial allowance, a headstone or marker, and even burial in a national cemetery for eligible veterans. These benefits honor the veteran's service and provide a final resting place that is dignified and respected.

Education benefits are also available to survivors. The VA offers the Survivors' and Dependents' Educational Assistance (DEA) program, which provides financial support for eligible spouses and children to pursue their educational goals. This benefit can help survivors build a brighter future and achieve their academic aspirations.

In addition to these specific survivor benefits, it is essential for families to be aware of the broader range of benefits available to veterans. These include healthcare benefits, housing assistance, employment and career benefits, disability compensation, financial assistance, home loan and mortgage benefits, small business and entrepreneurship benefits, and mental health and counseling services. Understanding and accessing these benefits can provide comprehensive support to veterans and their families, ensuring they have the tools and resources needed to thrive.

In conclusion, survivor benefits and support for families are crucial components of the comprehensive care provided to American veterans. These benefits aim to ease the financial, emotional, and practical burdens faced by survivors, ensuring they receive the support and assistance they deserve. By accessing these benefits, veterans and their families can find solace, stability, and a path towards a brighter future.

# Chapter 10: Home Loan and Mortgage Benefits for American Veterans

VA Home Loan Refinance Options for Veterans

One of the many benefits available to American veterans is the opportunity to refinance their home loans through the Department of Veterans Affairs (VA). This subchapter will explore the various VA home loan refinance options, providing valuable information to veterans and their families.

Refinancing a home loan can offer several advantages, such as lowering monthly payments, reducing interest rates, and accessing cash for other financial needs. For veterans who have served their country, the VA offers specific refinancing options tailored to their unique circumstances.

One popular VA refinance option is the Interest Rate Reduction Refinance Loan (IRRRL), also known as the VA Streamline Refinance. This program allows veterans to refinance their existing VA loan to obtain a lower interest rate without the need for additional documentation or a new appraisal. The IRRRL is an excellent choice for veterans looking to save money on their monthly mortgage payments.

Another option is the Cash-Out Refinance, which allows veterans to refinance their current mortgage for a higher amount than what they owe. This program is ideal for veterans who need funds to consolidate debt, make home improvements, or cover other expenses. With the Cash-Out Refinance, veterans can tap into their home equity and receive cash back at closing.

Additionally, veterans who have conventional or FHA loans can refinance into a VA loan through the VA Cash-Out Refinance program. This option offers the same benefits as the Cash-Out Refinance, allowing veterans to take advantage of the VA loan program's favorable terms and benefits.

It is essential for veterans and their families to understand these refinance options and consider them when evaluating their financial goals. Refinancing a home loan can provide veterans with significant savings, increased cash flow, and improved financial stability.

In conclusion, the VA offers several home loan refinance options designed to meet the unique needs of American veterans. Whether veterans are looking to lower their interest rates, access cash, or refinance from a non-VA loan, the VA has programs in place to assist them. By exploring these options, veterans and their families can make informed decisions to improve their financial situations and secure a brighter future.

Grant Programs for Home Adaptations and Accessibility

One of the challenges that many veterans and their families face is making their homes accessible and adaptable to their needs. Whether it's due to a disability or aging, home modifications can greatly improve the quality of life for veterans and their loved ones. Thankfully, there are grant programs available to provide financial assistance for these necessary changes.

The Department of Veterans Affairs (VA) offers several grant programs specifically aimed at helping veterans make their homes more accessible. One such program is the Specially Adapted Housing (SAH) grant, which provides funds to veterans with certain service-connected disabilities to construct or modify their homes to meet their unique needs. This grant can cover the costs of ramps, widened doorways, accessible bathrooms, and other necessary adaptations.

Similarly, the Home Improvements and Structural Alterations (HISA) grant is available to veterans with service-connected disabilities or veterans with non-service-connected disabilities. This program provides funds for home modifications that improve the veteran's access to essential facilities within their home, such as bathrooms, kitchens, and entryways.

In addition to the VA programs, there are also grant opportunities through nonprofit organizations and state agencies. The Disabled American Veterans (DAV) Charitable Service Trust, for instance, offers grants to disabled veterans for home modifications, including wheelchair ramps, stair lifts, and bathroom modifications.

To access these grant programs, veterans and their families must meet certain eligibility criteria. This typically includes proof of military service, documentation of disability, and an assessment by a healthcare professional. It's important to note that the application process for these grants can be complex and time-consuming, so it's advisable to seek assistance from a veterans service organization or a knowledgeable advocate to navigate the process successfully.

Making home adaptations and ensuring accessibility is crucial for veterans and their families to live independently and comfortably. These grant programs provide essential financial support to make these modifications possible. By taking advantage of these opportunities, veterans can create a safe and accessible living environment that meets their unique needs.

Overall, it's important for veterans and their families to be aware of the grant programs available for home adaptations and accessibility. These programs can significantly improve the quality of life for veterans with disabilities or aging-related challenges. By exploring these options and seeking assistance from relevant organizations, veterans can ensure that their homes are tailored to their needs and provide a supportive environment for their well-being.

Mortgage Assistance and Loan Forgiveness Programs

One of the many challenges that veterans and their families face is navigating the complexities of the housing market. However, there are several mortgage assistance and loan forgiveness programs specifically designed to support American veterans in achieving their homeownership goals. In this subchapter, we will explore these programs and the benefits they offer.

The Department of Veterans Affairs (VA) offers a range of home loan benefits to eligible veterans, including VA-backed loans with competitive interest rates and flexible terms. These loans are provided by private lenders, with the VA guaranteeing a portion of the loan, making it easier for veterans to secure financing. Additionally, the VA offers the Interest Rate Reduction Refinance Loan (IRRRL) program, which allows veterans to refinance their existing VA loan to obtain a lower interest rate.

For those veterans who are struggling to make their mortgage payments, the VA's Loan Guaranty Service provides foreclosure avoidance assistance. Through programs such as the VA Home Loan Modification and VA Home Loan Forbearance, veterans can explore options to modify their loan terms or temporarily suspend their payments to avoid foreclosure.

In addition to VA programs, there are also loan forgiveness initiatives available for veterans who work in public service or specific professions. The Public Service Loan Forgiveness (PSLF) program, for example, offers loan forgiveness to veterans who have made 120 qualifying payments while employed in a qualifying public service position. This can provide substantial relief for veterans burdened with student loan debt.

It is important for veterans to be aware of these mortgage assistance and loan forgiveness programs, as they can greatly alleviate the financial strain of homeownership and student loan debt. By taking advantage of these resources, veterans can secure affordable housing, avoid foreclosure, and potentially have their loans forgiven.

In conclusion, veterans and their families have access to a range of mortgage assistance and loan forgiveness programs designed to support their housing needs. Whether through VA-backed loans, foreclosure avoidance assistance, or loan forgiveness initiatives, these programs aim to make homeownership more accessible and affordable for American veterans. By understanding and utilizing these benefits, veterans can achieve their housing goals and create a stable foundation for themselves and their families.

Homeownership Counseling and Education for Veterans

As veterans and their families navigate the various benefits available to them, it is crucial to recognize the importance of homeownership counseling and education. This subchapter aims to shed light on the resources and support systems available to help veterans achieve their dream of owning a home.

Homeownership counseling and education programs provide valuable guidance and assistance to veterans at different stages of the home buying process. Whether you are a first-time homebuyer or looking to refinance an existing mortgage, these programs offer comprehensive information and personalized advice to ensure informed decision-making.

One of the key benefits of homeownership counseling is the access to financial guidance. These programs can help veterans understand their financial situation, assess their eligibility for home loans, and explore various financing options. By working closely with trained counselors, veterans can develop a realistic budget, establish a savings plan, and improve their credit score if needed. Additionally, veterans can learn about special loan programs specifically designed to meet their unique needs, such as the VA Home Loan program.

Education is another critical component of homeownership counseling. Veterans and their families can attend workshops and seminars that cover topics such as understanding mortgage terms, avoiding predatory lending practices, and maintaining a healthy financial profile. These educational sessions empower veterans to make informed decisions, negotiate favorable terms, and protect themselves from potential scams or frauds.

Furthermore, homeownership counseling programs often collaborate with housing agencies and community organizations to provide additional support. These partnerships may offer resources for finding affordable housing options, assistance with down payments or closing costs, and information on home maintenance and energy efficiency.

In conclusion, homeownership counseling and education programs play a vital role in helping veterans and their families achieve their homeownership goals. By providing financial guidance, education, and access to valuable resources, these programs empower veterans to navigate the complex process of buying a home. It is essential for veterans to take advantage of these services to ensure a successful and sustainable homeownership experience.

Homeless Prevention and Rapid Rehousing Assistance

One of the pressing issues faced by veterans and their families is homelessness. Many veterans struggle to find stable housing upon returning to civilian life, and this can have a detrimental impact on their overall well-being. However, there are several programs and resources available to help prevent homelessness and provide rapid rehousing assistance for American veterans.

The Homeless Prevention and Rapid Rehousing Assistance (HPRP) program is a vital resource designed to address the immediate housing needs of veterans who are at risk of becoming homeless or are already homeless. This program provides financial assistance to cover rental expenses, utility bills, and other costs associated with obtaining and maintaining stable housing.

Through the HPRP program, veterans and their families can receive short-term financial aid to prevent eviction, pay for security deposits, and cover moving expenses. This assistance is crucial in ensuring that veterans have a safe and stable place to call home, allowing them to focus on other areas of their lives such as employment, education, and healthcare.

In addition to the HPRP program, there are various other resources available to veterans in need of housing assistance. The Department of Veterans Affairs (VA) offers several programs that aim to provide affordable housing options for veterans, including the VA Home Loan program and the Supportive Services for Veteran Families (SSVF) program.

The VA Home Loan program helps veterans secure affordable mortgage loans to purchase or refinance their homes. This program offers favorable terms and conditions, making homeownership more accessible to veterans and their families. The SSVF program, on the other hand, provides case management services and temporary financial assistance to help veterans and their families quickly regain housing stability.

It is essential for veterans and their families to be aware of these housing benefits and resources. By taking advantage of these programs, veterans can find the support they need to secure and maintain stable housing. This, in turn, contributes to their overall well-being and allows them to focus on rebuilding their lives after military service.

In conclusion, homelessness is a significant issue that many veterans face. However, there are various programs and resources available to prevent homelessness and provide rapid rehousing assistance. By leveraging these resources, veterans and their families can find the support they need to obtain and maintain stable housing, leading to improved overall well-being and a better quality of life.

# Chapter 11: Small Business and Entrepreneurship Benefits for American Veterans

Overview of Small Business Benefits for Veterans

As a veteran or a family member of a veteran, you have made incredible sacrifices for our country. The good news is that there are numerous benefits available to you, including those related to small business and entrepreneurship. This subchapter will provide you with an overview of the various small business benefits that you can access.

One of the significant advantages for veterans interested in starting or expanding a small business is the availability of financial assistance. The Small Business Administration (SBA) offers loans and grants specifically tailored to veterans. These funds can help you with startup costs, equipment purchases, or even hiring employees. Additionally, the SBA provides training and counseling to ensure your business's success.

Moreover, the federal government has set a goal to award at least 3% of all federal contracting dollars to service-disabled veteran-owned small businesses. This provides an excellent opportunity for veterans to secure government contracts and expand their business.

In addition to financial assistance, veterans can also access educational resources to enhance their entrepreneurial skills. The SBA offers training programs, workshops, and online resources to help veterans develop business plans, understand market strategies, and navigate the complexities of running a successful small business.

Furthermore, being a veteran also opens doors to networking opportunities and mentorship programs. Various veteran-owned business organizations, such as the Veterans Business Outreach Centers

(VBOCs), provide support and guidance through workshops, counseling, and mentorship programs. These resources can help you connect with other veterans who have successfully established their businesses and learn from their experiences.

It is important to note that small businesses owned by veterans may also be eligible for preferential treatment in government procurement processes. This means that federal agencies may give priority to veteran-owned businesses when awarding contracts, providing a competitive advantage in the marketplace.

In conclusion, the benefits available to veterans interested in small business and entrepreneurship are vast. From financial assistance and educational resources to networking opportunities and preferential treatment in government contracts, these benefits are designed to support and empower veterans in their entrepreneurial endeavors. Take advantage of these resources and turn your business dreams into a reality.

Government Contracting Opportunities for Veteran-owned Businesses

One of the many benefits available to American veterans is the opportunity to secure government contracts for their businesses. The federal government has implemented programs and initiatives to support and promote veteran-owned businesses, providing them with a chance to thrive in the competitive marketplace. This subchapter will explore the various government contracting opportunities available exclusively for veteran-owned businesses and highlight the advantages veterans and their families can gain from these programs.

Government contracting can be a lucrative avenue for veterans looking to start or expand their businesses. The federal government spends billions of dollars each year on goods and services, and it actively seeks to award a certain percentage of these contracts to veteran-owned businesses. This preference is not only a way to honor and support veterans but also recognizes their unique skills, experience, and dedication.

To help veterans access these contracting opportunities, the government has established the Veterans First Contracting Program. This program requires federal agencies to set aside a portion of their contracts for veteran-owned small businesses (VOSBs) and service-disabled veteran-owned small businesses (SDVOSBs). By doing so, it ensures that veterans have a fair chance to compete and succeed in the federal marketplace.

To qualify for these set-aside contracts, veteran-owned businesses must go through a certification process, which verifies their veteran and ownership status. This certification is essential as it enables veterans to participate in the government's contracting programs and gain an edge over their competitors.

In addition to the Veterans First Contracting Program, there are other initiatives and resources available to support veteran entrepreneurs. The Small Business Administration (SBA) offers counseling, training, and access to capital through its Office of Veterans Business Development. This office provides veterans with the necessary tools and resources to start, grow, and manage their businesses successfully.

Moreover, the SBA's Service-Disabled Veteran-Owned Small Business Program provides additional contracting opportunities for service-disabled veterans. This program allows federal agencies to award sole-source contracts to SDVOSBs, streamlining the procurement process and providing veterans with an advantage in securing government contracts.

Overall, government contracting opportunities for veteran-owned businesses present a unique chance for veterans and their families to leverage their skills, training, and dedication to succeed in the business world. By participating in these programs and initiatives, veterans can access a wide range of benefits such as increased revenue, expanded networks, and the satisfaction of contributing to the nation's economy.

Veteran Business Development Programs and Resources

In addition to the various healthcare, educational, housing, and employment benefits, the United States government provides a range of programs and resources to support veterans and their families in starting and growing their own businesses. These initiatives aim to empower veterans and help them transition into successful entrepreneurs, leveraging their skills and experiences gained during their military service. This subchapter explores the various veteran business development programs and resources available to veterans and their families.

Small business ownership can be a fulfilling and rewarding career path for veterans. Recognizing this, the government has established several programs specifically tailored to assist veterans in starting, expanding, and managing their businesses. The Small Business Administration (SBA), for instance, offers a wide array of resources, including financing options, training programs, and counseling services. Veterans can benefit from SBA loan programs that provide favorable terms, such as reduced fees and interest rates, making it easier for them to access capital and grow their businesses.

Furthermore, the SBA's Office of Veterans Business Development (OVBD) focuses on assisting veterans, service-disabled veterans, reservists, and their dependents in navigating the complexities of entrepreneurship. The OVBD offers training and mentorship programs, workshops, and networking events to help veterans develop essential business skills and connect with industry experts and potential partners.

Additionally, many states and local communities have their own programs and incentives to encourage veteran entrepreneurship. These initiatives may include tax breaks, grants, and specialized training programs tailored to the unique needs of veterans.

Moreover, veteran-owned businesses can also benefit from preferential treatment in government contracting. The federal government has set a goal to award a significant percentage of contracts to veteran-owned small businesses. As a result, veteran entrepreneurs can take advantage of opportunities to secure government contracts, providing a steady and reliable source of revenue for their businesses.

By promoting veteran entrepreneurship, these programs and resources not only contribute to the economic well-being of veterans and their families but also drive innovation and job creation in local communities. Veterans and their families interested in starting or expanding their businesses should explore these valuable resources and take advantage of the support available to them.

In conclusion, the government recognizes the potential of veterans as entrepreneurs and offers a range of business development programs and resources tailored to their unique needs. From financing options and training programs to preferential treatment in government contracting, veterans and their families have access to numerous opportunities to start and grow their businesses. By harnessing their skills and experiences, veterans can embark on a fulfilling and successful entrepreneurial journey, contributing to their own financial well-being and the economic growth of their communities.

Access to Capital and Financing for Veteran Entrepreneurs

Starting a small business can be a daunting task for anyone, and veteran entrepreneurs face unique challenges when it comes to accessing capital and financing. However, there are various resources and programs available to help veterans and their families overcome these obstacles and turn their entrepreneurial dreams into reality.

One of the first steps in accessing capital is understanding the different financing options available. Traditional bank loans, Small Business Administration (SBA) loans, and grants are some of the common avenues veterans can explore. The SBA offers specific programs, such as the Veterans Advantage Loan Program, which provides guarantees on loans to veteran-owned businesses. This program can increase the likelihood of loan approval and improve the terms offered by lenders.

Additionally, there are numerous nonprofit organizations and foundations that provide financial assistance exclusively to veteran entrepreneurs. These organizations offer grants, loans, and mentorship programs tailored to the needs of veterans. They understand the unique challenges faced by veterans transitioning from military to civilian life and provide the necessary support to help them succeed in their business endeavors.

Furthermore, veteran entrepreneurs can tap into crowdfunding platforms as an alternative way to raise capital. Crowdfunding allows individuals to raise funds from a large number of people who believe in their business idea. This can be particularly beneficial for veterans, as their service often creates a strong sense of community and support.

It is also crucial for veterans to take advantage of educational resources and training programs specifically designed for veteran entrepreneurs. These programs can provide valuable insights into business planning, marketing strategies, financial management, and other essential skills needed to succeed in the competitive business world.

Lastly, networking and building connections within the veteran entrepreneur community can be invaluable. There are numerous veteran-focused organizations and associations that provide networking opportunities, mentorship, and access to potential investors and business partners.

In conclusion, while accessing capital and financing may pose challenges for veteran entrepreneurs, there are numerous resources and programs available to assist them. By leveraging these resources, veterans and their families can overcome financial barriers and turn their business ideas into successful ventures. Whether it is through traditional loans, grants, crowdfunding, educational programs, or networking, veteran entrepreneurs have the support they need to thrive in the world of small business and entrepreneurship.

Mentorship and Support Networks for Veteran-owned Businesses

Starting a business can be a daunting task for anyone, but for veterans transitioning into civilian life, it can present unique challenges. However, there are numerous mentorship and support networks available specifically designed to assist veteran-owned businesses in their journey towards success. In this subchapter, we will explore the invaluable resources and opportunities that exist to support veterans and their families in their entrepreneurial endeavors.

One of the most prominent organizations offering mentorship and support to veteran entrepreneurs is the Small Business Administration (SBA). The SBA provides a range of services, including business counseling, training programs, access to capital, and government contracting assistance. Through their Veterans Business Outreach Centers (VBOCs) located across the country, veterans can access one-on-one counseling, business plan development, and guidance on securing financing for their ventures.

In addition to the SBA, there are several nonprofit organizations dedicated to assisting veteran business owners. One such organization is the Institute for Veterans and Military Families (IVMF). The IVMF offers a variety of programs and initiatives, including the Entrepreneurship Bootcamp for Veterans (EBV), which provides experiential training in entrepreneurship and small business management.

Furthermore, veteran-owned businesses can benefit from joining industry-specific organizations that offer mentorship and networking opportunities. For example, the National Veteran-Owned Business Association (NaVOBA) connects veteran entrepreneurs with corporate partners, government agencies, and fellow veterans in their respective industries. These connections can lead to valuable insights, partnerships, and contracts that can help grow their businesses.

Moreover, many states have established their own programs to support veteran-owned businesses. These initiatives often include mentorship programs, procurement opportunities, and access to capital. By researching and connecting with these state-level resources, veterans can tap into additional support systems tailored to their specific region.

It is crucial for veterans and their families to take advantage of these mentorship and support networks to ensure their businesses thrive. By leveraging the expertise and guidance offered by these organizations, veteran entrepreneurs can navigate the complexities of entrepreneurship more effectively, increase their chances of success, and contribute to the economic growth of their communities.

In conclusion, mentorship and support networks play a vital role in empowering veteran-owned businesses. From the SBA and nonprofit organizations to industry-specific associations and state-level initiatives, there are numerous resources available to help veterans navigate the entrepreneurial landscape. By harnessing these networks, veterans and their families can leverage their skills, experiences, and military training to build successful businesses and create a brighter future for themselves and their communities.

Franchise and Entrepreneurship Training Programs for Veterans

For veterans and their families, transitioning from military service to civilian life can be a challenging process. However, there are numerous resources available to support veterans in their pursuit of successful careers and entrepreneurial ventures. One such avenue is through franchise and entrepreneurship training programs specifically designed for veterans.

Franchising offers veterans a unique opportunity to become business owners while benefiting from an established brand, proven business model, and ongoing support. Many franchises recognize the valuable skills and qualities that veterans possess, such as leadership, discipline, and a strong work ethic. As a result, they offer special incentives and training programs tailored to veterans.

These training programs aim to equip veterans with the necessary skills and knowledge to thrive in the business world. They cover a range of topics, including business planning, marketing strategies, financial management, and customer service. By participating in these programs, veterans can gain the confidence and expertise needed to launch and manage their own franchise.

Moreover, these programs often provide veterans with access to mentors send networking opportunities. Veterans can connect with successful franchise owners who can offer guidance and support throughout their entrepreneurial journey. Additionally, these programs facilitate networking events and conferences where veterans can meet industry experts and fellow veterans who share similar aspirations.

In addition to franchise opportunities, entrepreneurship training programs cater specifically to veterans interested in starting their own businesses from scratch. These programs provide comprehensive instruction on various aspects of entrepreneurship, including ideation, business planning, market analysis, and securing funding. Veterans can learn from experienced entrepreneurs and industry professionals who understand the unique challenges veterans may face.

By participating in franchise and entrepreneurship training programs, veterans can unlock a world of opportunities and achieve financial independence. These programs not only empower veterans to create their own successful businesses but also contribute to the overall economic growth of their communities.

As a veteran and family member, it is crucial to explore the wide range of benefits and resources available to you. This book aims to provide a comprehensive guide to healthcare benefits, educational benefits, housing benefits, employment and career benefits, disability compensation benefits, financial assistance benefits, mental health and counseling benefits, burial and memorial benefits, home loan and mortgage benefits, and small business and entrepreneurship benefits for American veterans.

Remember, you are not alone on your journey. There are organizations, government agencies, and fellow veterans ready to support you every step of the way.

# Chapter 12: Conclusion

Summary of Key Benefits and Resources

In "Serving Those Who Served: A Comprehensive Guide to Healthcare Benefits for American Veterans and Their Families," we aim to provide veterans and their families with a comprehensive understanding of the various benefits and resources available to them. This subchapter will summarize the key benefits that veterans can access in different areas of their lives, including healthcare, education, housing, employment, disability compensation, financial assistance, mental health and counseling, burial and memorial, home loans and mortgages, as well as small business and entrepreneurship.

Healthcare Benefits for American Veterans: The Department of Veterans Affairs (VA) offers a range of healthcare services, including primary care, specialized care, mental health care, and preventive care. Veterans can access these services at VA medical centers, community-based outpatient clinics, and Vet Centers.

Educational Benefits for American Veterans: The GI Bill provides educational assistance to veterans, helping them pursue higher education or vocational training. It covers tuition, housing allowances, and other educational expenses.

Housing Benefits for American Veterans: The VA offers various housing benefits, such as home loans with favorable terms, grants for adapting homes to accommodate disabilities, and assistance for homeless veterans to find stable housing.

Employment and Career Benefits for American Veterans: Veterans can access resources to aid in their transition to civilian employment, such as job training programs, career counseling, and priority hiring in federal government jobs.

Disability Compensation Benefits for American Veterans: Veterans who have service-connected disabilities can receive compensation to assist with the financial burdens associated with their disabilities. The VA provides disability ratings and monthly compensation payments based on the severity of the disability.

Financial Assistance Benefits for American Veterans: Veterans facing financial difficulties can access various forms of assistance, including pensions for wartime veterans, grants for disabled veterans, and loans for small businesses.

Mental Health and Counseling Benefits for American Veterans: The VA offers mental health services, including counseling, therapy, and treatment for conditions such as post-traumatic stress disorder (PTSD) and substance abuse.

Burial and Memorial Benefits for American Veterans: Veterans are eligible for burial in national cemeteries, with honors including a gravesite, headstone or marker, and a burial flag. Surviving family members may also receive benefits such as memorial services and financial assistance.

Home Loan and Mortgage Benefits for American Veterans: The VA provides home loan guarantees, making it easier for veterans to secure affordable mortgages. This benefit includes options for purchasing, building, or improving homes.

Small Business and Entrepreneurship Benefits for American Veterans: Veterans interested in starting or expanding their own businesses can access resources, training programs, and financial assistance through the VA and other government agencies.

By understanding and utilizing these key benefits and resources, veterans and their families can enhance their quality of life, access necessary healthcare, pursue education, secure stable housing, find meaningful employment, receive compensation for disabilities, receive financial assistance, improve mental health and counseling, honor fallen comrades, and achieve their entrepreneurial dreams. This subchapter serves as a gateway to exploring each benefit in more detail and accessing the necessary support to make the most of these opportunities.

Taking Action: Steps to Access and Maximize Benefits

As a veteran or a family member of a veteran, you are entitled to a range of healthcare, educational, housing, employment, and financial benefits. However, navigating through the complex system of benefits can often be overwhelming. This subchapter aims to provide you with a step-by-step guide on how to access and maximize the benefits available to you.

1. Identify your eligibility: Start by understanding the specific benefits you may be eligible for based on your service history, disability status, or other relevant factors. This will help you focus on the benefits that are most applicable to your situation.

2. Gather documentation: Collect all the necessary documents required to apply for benefits. These may include your military service records, medical records, discharge papers, and proof of relationships if you are applying as a family member. Having these documents ready will streamline the application process.

3. Research and seek assistance: Take advantage of resources available to help you understand the benefits and how to access them. Reach out to veteran service organizations, such as the Department of Veterans Affairs (VA), or consult with a Veteran Service Officer who can provide guidance and support throughout the process.

4. Apply for benefits: Submit your applications for the specific benefits you are seeking. Follow the instructions carefully and provide all

required information to avoid delays. Keep copies of all documents and correspondence for your records.

5. Connect with support networks: Engage with local veteran support groups and organizations that can provide additional resources and assistance. These networks can offer valuable insights, share experiences, and provide emotional support during your journey.

6. Maximize utilization: Once you have been approved for benefits, take full advantage of the services available to you. Schedule regular healthcare check-ups, explore educational opportunities, utilize housing assistance programs, and actively seek employment and career support.

7. Stay informed: Benefit programs and eligibility criteria can change over time. Stay up-to-date with the latest information by regularly reviewing official websites, attending workshops, and subscribing to newsletters or publications focused on veterans' benefits.

Remember, you are not alone in this process. Numerous organizations and individuals are dedicated to serving and supporting veterans and their families. By taking action, staying informed, and utilizing available resources, you can access and maximize the benefits you rightfully deserve.

Empowering Veterans and Their Families for a Successful Future

Introduction:

In this subchapter, we will explore the various ways in which veterans and their families can be empowered for a successful future. From healthcare and educational benefits to housing and employment opportunities, this section will provide you with a comprehensive guide to the resources available to American veterans and their families.

By understanding and utilizing these benefits, you can pave the way for a brighter and more prosperous future.

Healthcare Benefits for American Veterans:

As a veteran, you are entitled to a range of healthcare benefits that can ensure your physical and mental well-being. From comprehensive medical coverage to specialized services for conditions related to military service, these benefits can provide you with the care you need to lead a healthy life. Additionally, counseling and mental health services are available to address any emotional or psychological challenges you may face.

Educational Benefits for American Veterans:

Continued education is vital for personal growth and career advancement. American veterans and their families have access to a variety of educational benefits, including tuition assistance, scholarships, and vocational training programs. Whether you are looking to pursue a degree, learn a new skill, or gain certification in a specific field, these benefits can help you achieve your goals.

Housing Benefits for American Veterans:

Finding and maintaining suitable housing is essential for veterans and their families. From home loans and mortgage assistance to grants for home modifications, there are numerous programs available to help you secure affordable and safe housing. Additionally, rental assistance programs can provide temporary support if you are facing housing instability.

Employment and Career Benefits for American Veterans:

Transitioning from military service to civilian life can be challenging, but there are resources available to help you succeed in the job market.

Employment benefits for veterans include job placement services, career counseling, and training programs. Furthermore, there are specific initiatives to support veteran-owned businesses and foster entrepreneurship.

Disability Compensation Benefits for American Veterans:

If you have incurred service-connected disabilities, you may be eligible for disability compensation benefits. These benefits provide financial assistance to veterans who have suffered injuries or illnesses due to their military service. Understanding the claims process and accessing these benefits can significantly improve your quality of life.

Financial Assistance Benefits for American Veterans:

Financial stability is crucial for a successful future. American veterans and their families have access to various financial assistance programs, including pensions, grants, and loans. These benefits can help alleviate financial burdens and provide support during challenging times.

Mental Health and Counseling Benefits for American Veterans:

The mental health and well-being of veterans and their families are of utmost importance. There are numerous counseling services and support programs available to address the unique challenges faced by veterans, including post-traumatic stress disorder and substance abuse. By seeking help and utilizing these resources, you can ensure a healthier and happier future.

Burial and Memorial Benefits for American Veterans:

Honoring the service and sacrifice of veterans is a priority. Burial and memorial benefits are available to ensure a dignified final resting place for veterans. These benefits include burial allowances, markers or headstones, and memorial services to honor your service to the nation.

Home Loan and Mortgage Benefits for American Veterans:

Owning a home is a significant goal for many veterans and their families. Home loan and mortgage benefits specifically cater to the needs of veterans, offering competitive interest rates, low down payments, and flexible loan options. These benefits make homeownership more accessible and affordable.

Small Business and Entrepreneurship Benefits for American Veterans:

For those veterans interested in starting their own business, there are numerous resources and support programs available. Funding opportunities, mentorship programs, and government contracts specifically cater to veteran-owned businesses, providing the necessary tools and support for entrepreneurial success.

Conclusion:

As a veteran, you and your family are entitled to a wide range of benefits that can empower you for a successful future. From healthcare and education to housing and employment, these benefits are designed to support you in various aspects of life. By taking advantage of these resources, you can pave the way for a brighter and more prosperous future for yourself and your loved ones. Remember, your service to the nation is valued, and these benefits are a token of gratitude for your sacrifices.